# ADVANCE PRAISE

"*ER Doctor* is a wonderful peek into the personal life of a straight-talking ER physician, Paul Weinberg. Dr. Weinberg recounts some of his most memorable cases with precision and a dearth of adjectives. His fascinating array of cases range from headaches that turned out to be more; sodomy; finding a Twinkie wrapper in the fat folds of a 600 lb. woman; diagnosing the rare disease botulism, to patching up gunshot wounds. Being comprehensive, a few patients who sadly died before or when bought to the ER are included. Anyone who wants a real look into the practice of ER medicine, or into actual ER cases, should read this book."

**Steven C. Markoff**
Author, *The Case Against George W Bush*

"A page turner; I'm sure you will enjoy the read."

**Carl R. Chudnofsky, MD**
Professor and Chair
Department of Emergency Medicine
Keck School of Medicine of USC

Published by
**LID Publishing**
An imprint of LID Business Media Ltd.
LABS House, 15–19 Bloomsbury Way,
London, WC1A 2TH, UK

info@lidpublishing.com
www.lidpublishing.com

A member of:

# BPR ✸

businesspublishersroundtable.com

**Represented by Peter Beren**
Peter Beren
Member, AAR
Publishing Consultant & Agent
THE PETER BEREN AGENCY
email: peterberen@aol.com
Phone: (510) 821-5539
Skype: peterberenagency
Web Site: www.Peterberen.com

© Paul Weinberg, 2022
© LID Business Media Limited, 2022

Printed in the United States
ISBN: 978-1-911687-24-5
ISBN: 978-1-911687-25-2 (ebook)

Cover and page design: Caroline Li

PAUL WEINBERG, M.D.

# ER
# DOCTOR

## TALES OF
## AN EMERGENCY
## ROOM DOCTOR

MADRID | MEXICO CITY | LONDON
BUENOS AIRES | BOGOTA | SHANGHAI

# CONTENTS

# ACKNOWLEDGEMENTS

The practice of Emergency Room medicine and surgery has allowed a special insight into the ways of people across cultures, place and age. It was fulfilling in helping to understand this thing we call Life.

I am fully thankful for my training at LACUSCMC and the citizens of Los Angeles County, and the teachers who allowed me the first experiences of being a physician. They all provided the foundation for my life's career.

My agent Peter Beren, who said he had "a lot of faith" in my book. His encouragement came at just the right time and gave me the drive needed to push the project onward.

As always, I owe a great debt of thanks to A. R. Hawarden. A terrific force who kindly guided me into and through the complexity of getting a manuscript into a published book. I am very thankful for her guidance; without her efforts, this memoir would not have happened.

My wife Stacie, who nurtured and supported me through the times of stress and uncertainty.

Lily and Anna, my daughters, to whom this book is presented to share some insight into your father, and his work.

Friends and colleagues: Steve Markoff and Steve Gordon, Peter Anderson, Steve Morenz and Bob Cockrell, all from our original ER practice; David Stein and Bob Bushman. Each and every one who, in their own way, were air beneath my wings.

# PROLOGUE

Emergency room care will always be needed, desired and required.

In the face of pandemics and wars, the natural order of human illness and common accidents continues. Based on the laws of nature, the growth, development and decay of the human organism continues.

The ER is essential for getting initial medical needs addressed promptly.

The initial terrors patients and health care providers felt from the COVID virus have been diminished through experience, vaccines and increased population immunity.

However, the risks and deaths continue.

There could be another mutation of the virus, leading to unpredictable and unknown effects on virulence and contagiousness.

Fortunately, emergency medicine continues to be there for all, at all times.

My emergency room medicine tale in its own way is timeless, even against this present pandemic because the essential features of practice continue to be engaging, earnest and valid.

I have retired from emergency medicine and the ER.

Currently, I practice as medical director of an Aesthetic Medicine clinic.

The slope has changed.
However, the need for ER care will always be here.

**Paul Weinberg, MD**
Spring 2022

# INTRODUCTION

"Daddy, tell us a story that you worked on!"

That request from my kids was the starting point for many wondrous tales of the emergency room or ER. The details were designed to instruct about the basic human events – life and death, preventable drug and alcohol issues, psychiatric issues – and the errors behind them.

The stories generally were simple ones about minor wounds and abrasions caused by accident or in error. Common injuries occur accidentally and most of the stuff could have been prevented with just a little bit of common sense.

As an example, bicycle riding – a joyous activity of childhood that may be spoiled unless precautions are taken. Always ride a bicycle with closed-toe leather shoes to prevent nasty damage to your foot and toes from the chain or spokes when you fall. I taught my children to be sure to keep their feet well encased prior to riding and to always wear a helmet upon their growing young heads and brains.

I still remember the tragic case of a tall, fit young man brought in by the paramedics, deeply unconscious with a grave injury to his brain caused by a fall backward onto a curb edge while rollerblading. Preventable cases such as these are behind the worried parental warnings and those with experience in the emergency medicine (EM) department.

I would tell my kids these stories on the way to school when they were strapped into their car seats or waiting for dinner to be prepared while I decompressed with a cocktail. It seemed quite natural to discuss kitchen knife accidents while we were taking out the trash. These simple daily activities are an endless source of ER visits.

I also told the kids more sobering stories, like the patient whose throat was slashed open by a self-wielded knife. Whether an assault or an automobile accident, I had the uncommon privilege, experience or nightmare of being able to look into an open trachea, through which I easily inserted an endotracheal tube.

They were usually a little grossed out but not so impressed. From my standpoint, this was another notch in the belt of having seen too much.

I could have told so many ER stories had there been more memory and time. The kids were always asking about the most gruesome, most horrible and the worst ones. Sometimes I can remember those types of cases, other times it really is too difficult, and I try to block out those moments of practice.

The growing and collective erosion of chronic post-traumatic stress disorder (PTSD) has forced me to place my thoughts and emotions elsewhere. The children, unburdened by life, looked forward to these adventures and treated these stories almost like fairy tales, but in the ER, those dramas are acted out in real life.

The smell of blood is hard to explain. The language of smells is not very well defined except for the professionals (i.e., perfumers), and then the usual comparisons do not apply. The odor is not pleasant, something between mildly decaying meat and the sickly sweetness of rotting fruit, but for me, the associations are worse.

Large volumes of blood are never associated with pleasant things in the practice of EM. Patients are hurting, sprawled out and generally unstable and uncomfortable. They're on their way to unbeing and in a way, they are checking out.

The smell of blood, its mess, the pale color of the patient's skin, the trajectory all develop a final common pathway of care. The ER doctor needs to do their job correctly, carefully and promptly to save this life.

Technical knowledge is gained through training and study, but the experience of delivery is what matters. Intensity expands and contracts to the moment and situation. Sometimes it's imperative to focus on the entire patient and the whole process, and other times the focus is on a single body part.

Time will pass but it will not be apparent until it is all over or until there is breathing room again. Once you've resurfaced from this place, it's harder to fully be present again.

A portion of the self remains behind, and these encounters are cumulative daily across seasons, years and decades of practice. A stress disorder may creep in and erode the purity that all doctors go into the field of medicine attempting to uphold.

My entry into full-time EM practice was in 1976, at an aspiring community hospital in Orange County, California. Over the next many years, it would grow into a busy full-service hospital offering cardiac surgery, oncology, neonatal intensive care unit (ICU), pediatrics, a busy obstetrics and gynecology (OB-GYN or OB) service, and trauma service.

All types and severities of cases would present to the ER for evaluation. It was rare for a nonuniversity hospital to present a wide range of different cases, but it allowed me to develop a broad range of skills.

I did my part in keeping everyone I could alive, allowing patients to be further assisted by the other specialties with a shared goal of being fully restored to health.

Toward the end of the year of postgraduate training, I made the effort to develop the skills needed to keep patients alive. I practiced intubation and starting lines on all the patients and corpses that I could find to practice on, and I got good at it.

After a while, some ER doctors say they only want to take care of sunburns and fractured ankles. Those minor, self-limited conditions will not bore through one's mind and be replayed on a loop during quiet moments. Clean and simple seems better than desperate and complex. Daylight for darkness. Crisp and dry for bloody and festering.

One of my first jobs was in North Hollywood in a practice with many Church of Jesus Christ of Latter-day Saints believers. They were a healthy bunch: vegetarian, nonsmokers, no drinking and no bad habits. They were too quiet for my taste, medically speaking.

To keep up to date with my skills, I began moonlighting nights in ERs around L.A. County. There, I saw some medical action and felt more like the doctor I was trained to be. I preferred making major rapid improvements in patients' lives rather than managing the common medical problems like diabetes and high blood pressure.

I did not want to be a "slope jockey," a term for a physician who manages and slows the inexorable descent toward death, or an internist or that sort of subset of practitioners.

I gradually, then suddenly, stepped away from my family practice and into three decades practicing public EM.

Dealing with trauma patients fine-tunes common sense. Don't climb up on that ladder with or without the chainsaw, don't argue with too much intensity, handguns are best not handled, drive more slowly, don't drive when capacity is diminished, choose friends carefully and the bar to drink at with equal care, and temper passions.

As my kids grew, I left the urban ER full time and traveled the country and the world working with diverse patients and communities.

# CHAPTER 1

# THE JOURNEY

The delivery of medical care to the patient at the bedside comes in so many forms depending upon local culture, practitioner, experience, severity of illness and urgency.

My journey from medical student to mature and post-mature practitioner came after 30-plus years of experience. I certainly was a better physician at the end of my career than at its start, and that is a good thing.

Early on, particularly as a medical student, just the visual images and observation of the motions in giving care were quite sufficient. The different colors of body organs were quite amazing to see during the first experiences of observing a surgery.

The physical process of getting someone into the operating room was quite involved – moving a sick patient from the original bed onto a moveable stretcher to the operating room table and navigating through the halls, where the elevator was an effort in itself, so that then the more medical and surgical efforts would be able to start.

These views were a good beginning for a medical student. The learning was of the anatomy and physiology, biochemistry and pathology of the body. Basic building blocks of medicine. The feeling then was a bit like "drinking from a fire hose." Too much, too soon. Overwhelming.

And of course, with additional experience, remembering you had none, and training, the scene became more understandable.

As designed, by the end of your training these scenes were common and there was more of a feeling of understanding and control of these clinical situations. These feelings were real, but the genuine lack of experience made this an awkward time in the pathway to maturity of practice.

Initially, in the first two to five years of practice, the honeymoon period, I loved the practice of medicine so much that I would have done this work without pay.

My satisfaction from the delivery of care was its own reward – this would change. Fearlessly, I would stride toward the most severe and worrisome cases, eager and bold to deliver care, innocent in a way to the possibility of ill effects, a poor outcome, misdiagnosis or any complications.

Then, slowly, the boldness diminished. The carefree delivery was eroded and slowly replaced with an understanding that outcomes might not be all that was expected by the patient.

A dawning of a new period of practice was upon me. These feelings stayed with me throughout my career – the new age of vulnerability. There was an ebb and flow of my personal concerns regarding intensity of the case and outcome concerns. It even caused me to see myself as a victim of my own practice.

An alcohol-fueled major trauma, an uninsured patient or a preventable accident would cause me to feel vulnerable and exposed when the all too frequent bad outcome might lead to a successful malpractice suit. Their preventable problem became my difficult and unavoidable responsibility.

In fact, this did not happen. My cynicism with the situation was not helpful to the joy and ease of practice. Later, these feeling diminished and became absorbed into the background tension of daily practice.

Onward another decade and more, these ordinary burdens of practice had become the day-to-day background of work and thus incorporated into my life. Not forgotten but smoothed out by time and experience. Another part of the journey was developing.

Of course, medicine is a service industry. I realized slowly and surely that the patients I cared for needed my help. It would seem obvious, but the genuine needs of the patients became clear to me. So many turned to the ER for help that they could not get elsewhere. I became much more compassionate and giving.

I realized that they could not be helped elsewhere in our society. In a way, I slowed down and offered kinder and gentler care. It was well received. My focus was more on the discomforts of the patients and less on the mechanisms of the physical illness.

By now, generally, I had the nuts and bolts of treatment down. This change allowed me to recreate the human aspect of practice, and it again became engaging for me. These feelings tended to emerge whenever I practiced in a more rural area, where knowledge and experience mattered. You were a bigger fish in a smaller pond and not just another MD in a county of 40,000 MDs.

Fortunately, the end of my career was in smaller and more rural areas, and these more pleasant feelings were the ones that were with me at the end. It was an excellent journey.

ER practice is composed of multiple "snapshots" (patients) that present in no particular order. This is repeated. The practitioner's growth comes with many encounters, repeated, not from a construction of encounters.

Viewed with a sufficiently large scale, the snapshots create a pattern that is not random but sufficiently irregular that it can seem random. You cannot really predict who or what the next patient will be needing in the way of care. However, from a distance you can see that there is some sort of pattern. Day, night, winter, summer, male, female, young and old, infectious, noninfectious, medical, surgical. The variety of the possibilities are much greater than the menu choices at a restaurant; logistical planning is much more difficult. I have tried to arrange these random snapshots of life in the ER to focus on the broader themes and experiences that I found meaningful as I look back on my journey.

# CHAPTER 2

# WELCOME TO THE ER

Emergency medicine in America is a critical asset to our healthcare system. The ER doctor is located at the interface of the public and the first point of healthcare.

If a doctor is needed outside of office hours, nights or holidays, if the patient is uninsured or has inadequate insurance, or is of such a social state that they might be unpleasant to be around, no one is turned away from the ER.

The person struggling with opioid addiction, the unkempt person, the person with an alcohol problem, the criminal, the mentally deficient, the houseless, those with poor language skills, emotionally disturbed, or generally toward the bottom of the social ladder – everyone receives the same care in an ER.

Pain in any part of the body or a weird feeling may also land a patient in the ER with everyone else who is falling off the wellbeing curve. A victim of an accident, a crime, or bad luck may also end up in the ER. The net of the ER is very wide, with a fine mesh that endlessly captures willing and unwilling patients.

Around 11:00 a.m. is a time when the ER is very busy, particularly on a Sunday or the third day of a holiday weekend. I didn't understand the phenomenon until I had my own family.

It would take us from waking at about 7:00 a.m. until 11:00 a.m. to get everything together and leave the house. The activities of daily living – cleaning, dressing, feeding and driving – took hours to complete. The four hours of phase-shifting works the same way in the evenings, too.

People go to bed between 10:00 and 11:00 p.m. to be at their jobs around 8:00 to 9:00 a.m. The evening at the ER does not get quiet until 1:00 to 2:00 a.m. most nights and may be busy again as people try to get in early with a complaint prior to going to work. In an urban area, the ER is so overutilized that it is busy at almost all hours of the day and night.

In an effort to protect my children from the nastiness of the night shift, I was quite strict in making them go to sleep on time around 9:00 p.m. I let them know that there was increased secretion of growth hormone during the sleeping hours and that they needed the extra sleep for their normal growth and development.

During the winter it worked just fine, but in the spring and summer with the increased daylight it was not possible to get them to bed on my schedule, and I did not even try.

The entire diagnostic spectrum of medicine and surgery can present at any time and any place. Certain illnesses and diseases have their own times and seasons. For example, ski-type injuries are rarely seen outside of skiing season. The athletic injuries follow the sports seasons.

There is a pattern to illness, also. Influenza and pneumonia cases are more common in winter. Some diarrhea cases are more common in summer. There is even a temporal pattern to cases. Some cases present in the morning and others in the evening.

As an example, when peoples' lungs fill up with fluid, known as acute pulmonary edema, that type of case almost always happens on the night shift. Medication refills are day-shift cases. Fevers can be day or night.

I cannot remember seeing a case of croup past 9:00 a.m. and earlier than 8:00 p.m. Congestive heart failure rarely presents during the day and is more usually diagnosed and treated in the evening. CVA or stroke typically presents in the morning when the patient is discovered after an evening of sleep.

The more unifying variables are the very young and the very old, where the extremes of life are represented. The old tend to suffer from chronic disease and the very young suffer from infectious diseases.

Those in the middle (age 16 to about 40) are the caregivers and would mostly show up due to diseases of abuse, passion, greed and violence. The productive years of life, in an economic and social sense, are often diluted by the need to care for people, knowing that life is a cycle and being aware of what's to come.

It is just as common to present to the ER with great insurance or with any condition that a personal physician thinks might be just a little unstable.

There are many reasons patients are referred to the ER by their providers. More often than not, medical necessity is not at the top of the list. Convenience, liability, complex, difficult patients, lack of surgical skill, time constraints, financial burden, golf games, and psychiatric patients are all shifted, shunted and sent to the ER.

In private practice, slow cash flow can be devastating; therefore, the ER becomes the safety valve for the community and society in general. I learned to just say "yes" to the calls referring all manner of patients to the ER without asking too many questions, particularly the pointed ones. After all, I know I am part of the great medical economic stream.

The physicians who send their cases to us sometimes refer simple cases they could have handled during the week. No case is too little or too uncomplicated to be referred to us for care during the weekend. They don't consider efficiency, and the effort and responsibility are referred away.

I suppose the process is similar to stock and bond traders. They do not wish to have exposure during the weekend when they do not have control of their portfolios. They choose not to have any open conditions during the weekend, so they consolidate their positions prior.

I can't blame the doctors who refer their patients to us. Why take a chance? They would rather be safe than sorry, and would only have more work, not more money, before the weekend begins.

Friday, for most people, is an easing of work and the beginning of leisure and rest. In the ER, it is a time of increased stress and chaos that usually begins shortly after noon.

From an operational standpoint, Friday afternoons and evenings in the ER are filled with nonessential cases that require the usually long and redundant workups. They are managed with tiny increments of care until they can again be cared for on Monday by the more knowledgeable referring physician.

The additional burden placed on the system by the recreational habits of the patients is not to be understated. Consider the "accidents" of the weekend warriors – motor accidents, drinking, recreational drug use and spousal abuse.

Three-day holiday weekends are even worse. By Monday, the crowds of citizens are wild, panicked and unruly in their need to be seen by physicians. The waits have greatly lengthened, the staff is more fatigued, and the overall effort and confusion are increased.

Frequently, the staff on the weekend is not the usual team but is made up of anyone with a license who needs or is forced to work on the weekend or the holiday. In these situations, there is a lessening of the efficiency of work and an increase in the frequency of errors made by the staff.

Staff members unfamiliar with the protocols of practice and the location of essential items of emergency care may cause the full-time staff to work harder. The regular staff members must do their own jobs as well as teach the "newbies."

The physicians on call for the weekend are not familiar with the patients they are responsible for, and that leads to another source of errors and poor outcomes.

Even the physicians on staff at the hospital use the ER for themselves and their patients. The usefulness of the ER to other doctors is legendary; we can do their work for them to a very large extent, and they can leave their concerns and the liability of their patient to someone else. We like to joke that referring physicians sleep better at night than ER physicians.

The ER offers the essential tests and attention of physicians at all times of the day or night without any concern regarding cost or authorization. Show up, get seen and, at least in the ERs I've worked in, get diagnosed and treated at a very high level of accuracy. The ER, with its commandment of care for all, represents democracy in action.

# CHAPTER 3

# WHILE YOU ARE SLEEPING

One evening, around the time I retired in 2008, I went to the self-serve gas station after dinner at the local all-you-can-eat Chinese buffet, the family feeling close and full and satisfied. My old Mercedes, close to 200K miles, is diesel and needed a fill-up. At the pump across the island stood a young Paso Robles patrol officer just starting his night shift.

We said hello. Talking with him brought back a flood of emotions related to my EM career and particularly the night shift. We commiserated over the pain of working during these hours. We joked that the hours of 2:30 to 5:30 a.m. were the worst as the light of day was so far away.

We both knew about the people, the problems, the emptiness and sadness of those whom we interact with in these hours. He said he had worked the night shift for some time and liked it because of the action and the "realness" of the work.

As we talked, I could feel my own tension returning. The memories and the feelings were still there. Surprisingly, a small part of me wanted to return to the scene but only for a short period of time. The thought of it would be better than the return to that reality.

I had learned a lot about how police think and operate, and how they handle criminals and victims just by existing in the same world. Over time, I have made good friends with some of the local officers that I interacted with on my night shift.

I respected them and the difficulty of their work. I related to the responsibility of having to make critical decisions with not enough time or data, and then being subject to intense review by superiors who may or may not be supportive. It's a tough job, and I worried a little about the future of this vigorous young officer. We both knew the same world, only through different angles and lenses.

EM physicians are more like police officers and less like firefighters. The group mentality of firefighters is rarely applied in the ER. We often make the most important decisions alone. Only on the more complex and slowly evolving cases do we obtain a friendly consultation. It is reassuring to get help with a troubling case under severe time constraints.

The officer and I said our goodbyes.

"Be safe," he said.

As I drove off with my family, I started to remember some of the categories of cases I had taken on during the night shift.

———————

As an EM physician, almost half the work takes place during the darkest hours. ERs do not close, and, in my busy urban practice, there was little time to sleep during night shifts. I have visited those late hours too much, and it has not been good for my emotional wellbeing.

Big-time motor vehicle accidents, and I mean big wrecks, arrive in the early morning after the bars and after-hours places close. As the darkness goes, there is often an extremely intoxicated driver involved in a crash. The blood alcohol levels in these cases are easily four to five times the legal limit of intoxication. The "victims" are hardly aware of what's going on and they don't smell great, either.

There is nothing like the night shift to reveal the unknown side of life. For most people, the hours of late darkness – from 11:00 p.m. to 5:00 or 6:00 a.m. – are not well known, only explored on New Year's Eve, a long airplane flight or in the face of an emergency.

The darkness of the night shift brings with it the domestic violence, drug overdoses, suicide attempts, severe alcoholic intoxication, shootings, stabbings, assaults of all types and sudden eye pains (the dilating pupil contributes to increased pressure within the eye).

Delay, neglect and decay are also the hallmarks of the night shift. The lacerations are longer, the wounds more delayed in presentation, and the patients crankier, less sanitary, articulate and educated.

The first battle for the night begins with the fatigue and bodily disruption of a disturbed circadian rhythm. This rhythm controls aspects of many cellular functions and as the cells go, the body goes too. Memory becomes impaired, the body feels tired, beat-up and cold.

One morning, very early, I was called by the nursing staff to evaluate a young male in his mid-20s who was mentally unstable. There was no visible acute or severe distress; however, he was "howling" like a wolf.

He was thin with a full head of long, dark, unkempt hair and had a long, dirty beard. His head was thrown back as he howled something unintelligible.

Despite my lengthy education and having the power of my profession and the strengths of the hospital behind me, I couldn't help but feel the small hairs on the back of my neck stand up.

This primitive response was powerful and unexpected and made me feel like he was in an otherworldly state that I couldn't quite put my finger on. From a medical standpoint, all he needed was some reassurance and sedation, then he was able to sleep comfortably for the rest of the night.

I still have a sharp memory of the event. I remember it as a skulking, dark, dreamlike sequence that felt like a glimpse into less civil times, when blood and force ruled societies.

The vast majority of people are obligate day timers awakened by daylight and asleep after it gets dark. On camping trips or during extended times without electricity, I have gone to sleep about 45 minutes after dark and then awakened at dawn. This has always felt good to me.

This is a strange new world waiting to be explored by anyone unfamiliar with the night shift. A visit to the waiting room of a busy ER during the early morning hours provides a glimpse into the surrounding community in a whole new light. The variety and range of the people waiting will open the mind and eyes to the more hidden lives of the locals.

I used to ask people, "Why did you come to the ER now?" during the early morning hours between 2:00 and 5:00 a.m. From a medical standpoint, these people were stable and had no urgent need to be seen. I finally stopped asking.

There was always some reason that finally revolved around fear – the hours of darkness, isolation and loneliness – the kind of things that could have been eased with a shot of whiskey, petting a dog, snuggling a warm body, chocolate or even a readjustment of the circadian rhythm through light therapy. The reason I stopped asking was because I knew their pain and emptiness from the many times I, too, had stayed up into the wee hours learning the practice of medicine.

However, in urban areas, there is so much nightlife that there are an equal number of people awake during the day and night. Ask any cop or ER worker, the night-crawlers are a different bunch. In general, they are not as civilized as the day-timers. They have a different rhythm and sense of ethics.

A classic night shift case is delusions of parasitosis. These "buggy" patients usually present about 2:00 to 3:00 a.m. with concerns of a skin itch; they feel like something is getting into and under their skin and they cannot get it out. It really bothers them, to the point of obsession.

Sometimes they'll even bring in a little piece of what it is that is bothering them wadded up in paper for examination, but magnification has never shown anything but scraps of skin debris.

It turns out that in the overwhelming majority of these cases, the patient has a substance use disorder involving cocaine or meth. The drug's effect on the brain is deluding the patient. Even when they show a positive urine test for drugs and this is carefully explained to the patient, they do not believe the explanation.

Most of the time, night shift patients could be described as somewhat off. Many of my night shift patients would make folks glad to have doors with locks and police around. Of course, they are interesting – interesting to assess, understand and observe their situations – but only for the length of a visit.

Other common night shift cases are abdominal pains. Certainly, this can be a serious problem of medical and surgical worry, but just as many turn out benign.

A careful history and physical, laboratory, X-ray and ultrasound evaluation in many of these cases do not come up with any cause of the patient's illness. They are given supportive care and discharged. It boggles my mind to think of the wasted healthcare dollars that are spent on these cases.

The memories of my feelings during the hours of 2:30 to 5:30 a.m. are not comforting or pleasant. The necessity to work those hours began to wear me down over time. The intensity of the unpleasant feelings increased over the years until it was almost intolerable. I began each night shift filled with dread, dread over my own anticipation of what would occur in the unpleasantness of the early morning hours.

Some nights, it felt as though daylight would never return. Over time I was able to monitor my feelings better and understood why I was feeling the way that I was, but it ultimately did not ease my worry about working during these hours. The tension is somewhat eased by knowing the plan for what's ahead.

One thing that got me through a night shift was working with a team. The condensing of the human spirit causes some ER doctors to lose compassion and therefore provide less thorough care. The feeling of wanting to curl up and throw in the towel is greatly eased by the life-giving force of the ER team. Almost always, that team includes the regular night shift workers.

The folks who have been phased into the night shift are able to continue the basic operations despite the lateness of the hours. They sleep during the day and in multiple catch-as-catch-can episodes. Most of the time, choosing this shift is an economic necessity – it may be better pay, a second job or ease the burden of a childcare responsibility – and they are getting through it until something better comes along.

These folks are the majority of the night shift workers. They do it for a while and then move on. Sometimes they choose the night shift to avoid interaction with family or, more commonly, other staff or administration, as there are no bosses during the night shift to bug them.

The rarest night shift workers are the natural night owls. They prefer the night shift because it suits their circadian rhythm. There are ER doctors who are not only alert and awake at 3:00 a.m. but are also cordial and helpful and happy.

The endless variety of presentations, even the most common cases, and the timing and rate of patient presentation, are part of what keep the ER such an intense and exciting place. This is why it has been the basis of multiple TV shows.

Everyone always asks me about the worst case I've ever seen, the oddest case and the wildest people. EMs rival the police in regular interesting and crazy dealings with the public. Though, with enough experience and time in the ER, the allure of the irregular does become inane, particularly when working the night shift.

There is also a magic to that rhythm, which can resolve feelings of darkness, negative space and depression as the body syncs up with the daylight once more.

Anyone can do a day shift. Usually, there isn't as much pain during the day, although the entire practice of EM is filled with pain and all its variations. Patients overwhelmingly come to the ER with complaints of pain. "It hurts," they say, and then start to tell their stories.

The only known variable is the duration of the shift. The effort will be over when the shift is completed, and the amount of effort is driven by the number of patients and the complexity and severity of their illnesses.

# CHAPTER 4

# THE GOLDEN SHOULDER

Since ERs are required to admit anyone, they are often the landing spot for people in trouble, with a low threshold of referral. It is a good starting place for their pinball-type journey to a more stable place of care.

The ER team reluctantly does its duty with their usual can-do attitude. Patients are given a physical and biochemical evaluation, started on treatment, stabilized, housed and fed, then launched into the swirl of psychiatric care paths.

Sometimes this can take hours and days, literally, of staff administrative time in trying to find placement. At least they are off the street, and safe from causing harm to themselves or the public.

I confess I have had frustration and anger in caring for people who were causing self-harm. For me, the most difficult are patients who smoke. My parents both smoked, suffered and gave away years of life due to that addiction. Living in a household of smokers also contributed to my asthma.

As a young teenager, I read the first Surgeon General's report on the health effects of smoking and pleaded with my parents to stop smoking. Now that I am a parent, I can see what a difficult position I put them in at that age by begging them to stop smoking.

In EM practice, the patients are usually seen only once for a particular problem. The habits that contribute to their recurrent illness are not dealt with by the EM physician. Emergency medicine care is not comprehensive across time.

I would counsel younger patients who came in with mild symptoms related to smoking. I gently teased them with a sense of irony by telling them how "brave" they were to smoke. They usually grinned in a somewhat sheepish manner and said they would try to stop.

I would tell the wheezing smoker that the unique sound in their lungs was their lungs' whispering plea for them to stop smoking. It made me feel just a bit better, more like a dad than a physician, that I could have contributed to them giving quitting a second thought.

Those struggling with alcohol misuse do not bother me nor do the drug users. Caring for them is easy in that I need to just treat them in a medical model. Each disease has a usual algorithm that defines the treatment and that is what they receive.

---

Once, a woman came to the ER cradling her left breast. The swollen breast was so very painful that even the slightest movement caused her pain. She called it "Billy." Now, "Billy" was sick, having been injected with heroin, and had swollen to the size of her head.

With a scalpel, I cut through the skin into the cavity and then allowed almost a cup of the foulest-smelling pus to drain out of her body. Fortunately, she left feeling better, never to be seen again.

Narcotics addiction is a serious and significant illness and needs to be treated as such. These patients are typically not receptive to treatment at the time that they present to the ER; they are there out of economic necessity and have made up a reason that would require treating them with narcotics, either a shot or pills, anything that they can take with them.

Unfortunately for many of those with substance use disorders, the endless question is, "Where do I get my next fix?"

These patients tend to be unusually self-serving and not forthcoming in giving a history. The history is essential for scale and insight into the scope and magnitude of their problem.

With an inaccurate and often fraudulent history, a physical examination becomes paramount for the doctor to sort out fact from fiction. With training and experience, the exam becomes a very useful tool in the undeclared battle between truth-seeking physicians and less fortunate patients.

There is a quiet and endless battle between ER physicians and those with substance use disorders. I have not met an ER physician who likes giving out narcotics when they are not needed, and, with experience, the physician gets good at sorting out the legitimate patient from someone looking for a fix.

Some patients have the "golden shoulder," a chronically subluxated shoulder, that they could pull out of joint on their own and then present to the ER as a shoulder dislocation. A shoulder dislocation is a painful condition often requiring narcotics to allow the shoulder to be relocated back into the joint, and patients who can dislocate at will are able to present themselves for narcotic treatment anytime, anyplace. They could get a shot for the reduction and then some pills to go for the pain that comes later.

One evening, this type of patient, commonly a younger male, presented to the ER with the complaint and history of a shoulder dislocation. My experience and some subtle clues from the X-ray let me know he had a substance use disorder.

I could not see myself treating him in the usual way with a shot in the butt and some pain pills to go. There had to be some other way to manage his shoulder pain.

Then I remembered something I had read in an orthopedic textbook from long ago that I had to look up again to jog my memory. I would treat him in a gentle, kind and painless manner as I cared for his shoulder, and I would not treat him with narcotics.

My treatment was to inject a local anesthetic directly into the shoulder joint, filling that volume with the liquid anesthetic that would totally take any pain away. It was a nonnarcotic solution to his complaint.

Following a careful sterile preparation to the shoulder, I injected the local anesthetic, and when it had worked its magic, I pushed his shoulder easily back into place. It was taken care of in a very slick manner.

The patient had what he ostensibly came in for corrected and I was glad that I did not contribute to his disorder. The patient had been treated and left, surprised at the solution but not able to complain about the failure to get narcotics. Today, a medical treatment for narcotics addiction might be offered, such as naltrexone or buprenorphine or another medication-assisted treatment (MAT).

In the ER, almost anything can happen, and sometimes it does. There are times in everybody's life when things get a little out of control and it's difficult to know why or how it happened. Sometimes, it is the role of the ER physician to put it all back together again and lead their patients back to someplace stable, grounded and normal.

It was another of those paramedic runs during the early hours in the morning, around 5:30 a.m. After being up all night dealing with the usual and unusual stuff of the urban scene, I was exhausted and numb enough that I was ready for anything.

The paramedics had the gray look of too many runs and too little sleep that night and could not wait to drop their patient off and scurry back to the station for some rest. They had been called by the boyfriend after his girlfriend had a seizure.

"Take care of it, Doctor."

The patient was not helpful either; she was still out of it from her seizure. Her vital signs were stable, however, and she was not currently seizing. I checked her briefly and she was all right for the moment. I sent off the labs and X-ray and sat down with the boyfriend to try to make sense of this case. He was doing better than his girlfriend. He could give some information, although it wasn't very clear. The drugs were wearing off, and he could make better sense of it now. I asked for some history.

"Diabetes? A previous history of seizure, allergies? What was going on when she had the seizure?" I asked.

"Not much," he said. "We were doing it." By that, he meant sexual intercourse, which is not a common cause of seizure.

"Like what else was going on?" I asked again.

They had been up all night like the Chicago song "25 or 6 to 4" says, and they had decided to do more coke. As a grand finale, perhaps he thought as a gift of love, he took the remaining powder, a good amount, and lustily applied it all to his girl's "yaya" (vaginal mucosa) with his hand.

The large surface area of highly vascular mucus membrane allowed a rapid absorption of drug and caused her to seize. With a nurse in attendance and the cooperation of the patient, who was now awake, I did a pelvic exam.

There were still a few white crystals present, no hidden drug packets inside, and no injury. When she felt well, she was good to go. He was relieved, and she was relieved. After the obligatory observation period, lab and X-ray evaluation, and the antidrug use lecture, they left hand in hand.

---

Another brief and unusual case I was involved in was well defined by the impulsiveness of a young man. He was in the ER for a repair of a laceration of his arm; there was nothing too alarming or unusual about the case, yet.

The usual procedure for wound repair is to start by cleaning the skin and then injecting lidocaine, a pain-killer, into all the wound edges to make the wound insensible and numb. The wound is then carefully explored for foreign bodies, cleaned and irrigated with high-pressure saline solution, then closed or pulled together with suture material. End of repair, just put a dressing on the freshly repaired wound and discharge the patient, with the correct aftercare instructions.

What becomes of the used supplies? They are gathered up by the nursing staff and disposed of in secure and safe containers.

In this case, in the few moments between my leaving the bedside and the disposal of items, this patient grabbed the syringe that contained some of the unused and still sterile lidocaine, pulled up his sleeve into a tourniquet, stuck the needle into the big vein of his elbow and pushed the entire contents into his body.

"Wow!" I said to myself. There was a possibility for a big-time event if there had been more of the active ingredient available, but I knew this, and he didn't. Nothing would happen; he would not get high or numb. The only sensations would be the spinning excitement of his mind and the little prick of pain in his elbow.

---

Another patient, dressed in all black, heavily tattooed, with a light mist of sweat on his pale and increasingly blue face, had just been hoisted onto the examination table. Limp and sprawled, he needed prompt, immediate and correct attention before he went into cardiac arrest. The diagnosis was pretty simple, even if his wife was not forthcoming with his immediate and past history.

She knew or should have known that it was not the "seizure" that she told us about nor the fall a week or so earlier that set this thing off. I pulled up his eyelids and saw the giveaway sign of equal tiny pupils. They were small, like eyes get in bright sunlight. These tiny dark spots told the story: an opioid overdose.

Treatment was easy – we needed to help him breathe until the reversing agent had a chance to work. The nurse did the excellent job of finding a vein and the agent was injected.

Miraculously, and almost instantly, he awakened and denied the drug use. With a little talking to and some time, he admitted to the heroin use. We found out that this was the fourth time he had almost died. His lack of concern was sobering.

He passed the basic ER metabolic screen, was treated very well, and was coaxed to stay until it was safe for him to leave. He left after ignoring my educational lecture on lifestyle choices. His wife cared almost as little as he did.

A medical background does not inoculate against this type of illness, unfortunately.

There has always been tension between inexperience and wisdom, youth and age, fearless and fearful, and invincible with the "can't happen to me" attitude versus the "seen it all happen" attitude. An EM physician is at the intersection where all these contrasts collide. ER physicians have seen it all, maybe too much, and that makes them feel older than their age. Family, at home, usually does not understand that type of knowledge.

My children did well through their worrisome development years when many teens experiment with drug and substance use. The stories I told them, and their own minor experimentation, have kept them on the straight side of life.

I know personally of two families with physician parents whose children, raised similarly, took very different paths. In each case, one child followed the safer path and the other took a walk on the wild side, even though there were no preexisting mental or drug issues in these homes. Then there are the children of addicts.

———————

The EMS radio crackled with the warning that they were bringing in an unresponsive young female with a worrisome reduction of vital signs. They were continuing to give the usual protocol therapy of airway, CPR and drugs but not much was improving. Narcan, a reversing agent for opioid overdose, didn't do anything either.

Deathly pale and just a little moist, unmoving and unconscious upon being transferred to the gurney from the ambulance stretcher, she continued to need medical care. Her electrocardiogram (EKG, a machine that measures and displays the electrical signal from the heart) was flatline except for the carefully timed CPR artifact of the technician. Without that effort, the sensitive EKG heart monitoring showed that she was electrically dead.

No surprise was coming, there was no miracle, and shortly after some additional resuscitation, I made the necessary decision to pronounce her dead right there in the ER. I asked that she be disconnected from any monitoring devices.

I instructed the nurses, "Make her look nice so the family can view her but leave the ET tube in because the coroner demands that. I'll explain it to the family." The endotracheal tube (ET) is a flexible main breathing tube inserted into the trachea to allow artificial ventilation.

The family members and friends are kept apart from the treatment area in any available open treatment room. When I entered, all eyes were on me with hope. The cast of soon-to-be mourners from left to right: mother, daughter, sister of fiancé and fiancé, who spoke first.

"She had been clean for so long, she was doing so well, four months, and when I came back from the QuickShop she was like that, gray, looking bad, so I called 911. No, I didn't give CPR. I didn't know how, and I was afraid."

I looked at the other adults, and they indicated agreement. The daughter, physically about 14 and mature for her age with a woman's face and physical development, just observed. I glimpsed her future now. She was going to be raised by the addict's mother and quickly released into adulthood. Let her find her way home later and hopefully, she will find her own path.

Sadly, I told them the news of the patient's death. Another heroin overdose death in this tiny Ohio town, close to ground zero in our national epidemic of opioid abuse. The couples embraced tearfully. I invited them to view her, and they agreed. I faded from the room, shaking my head.

I had seen this too many times.

Some of the toughest patients in medicine to comfort and manage are pain patients, those unfortunate people whose lives are dominated by pain. Pain and complaints of pain are extremely common presentations of patients into the healthcare system and the ER as well. For too many, we are the first place, last place or only resort.

There is a whole specialty directly involved in the care of these patients: pain medicine. They are highly trained and skilled physicians who do an enormous amount of good.

We take all who come, of course. These patients are taken care of and handled well in the ER. We get so much practice with difficult pain patients that usually ER physicians become on-the-job experts at pain management.

———————

Then there is the abuse of alcohol, and physician families, once again, are not immune from its effects.

A glib, charming wife dying of liver disease was patiently brought to the hospital by her husband, whom I had known for years, ever since his earlier training in podiatry during residency at the hospital. He was straightforward, sincere, diligent and knowledgeable. He also seemed to be just a little naïve.

He did not know that this would be her last admission. His knowledge of medicine was not sufficient to know the gravity of her illness. I felt drawn into the scene and sad that she was so very ill.

His wife was charming and beautiful, powerful in that social currency of men and women, smiling and chatty to the extent that it was a bit hard to get a history from her, but her husband gave the facts. Nicely dressed and carefully made up, she radiated charm, but her physical appearance gave me a clue that something was wrong. This glamorous woman had let the dark roots of her blonde hair grow too long. She had been unable to attend to them, a tip-off that something was not right. The other and more important clues were the signs of alcoholic liver disease. Her eyes were like yellow searchlight beacons; the whites of the eye had turned yellow, and her unkempt hair was a time marker on the road to death.

In fact, when I got some of the laboratory values back, her blood alcohol level was above the legal level for intoxication. The husband did not have a clue. She acted as the child and he the parent who had to bring her to the hospital for care. I asked to speak with him privately.

"Your wife is very ill, and I do not think she will live very much longer," I told him. He was not stunned by the news but wasn't able to accept it either.

He asked a few questions and we returned to her bedside. I made further arrangements for admission, and she was quietly brought to a private room for care. She passed away of end-stage liver disease a few days later in the hospital.

I wondered what their courtship and marriage were like. The excitement of marriage at its beginning; then the realization of the heavy burden of living with an alcoholic, the drowned hope of a cure, and the decline at the end as she slid into a stupor, coma and then death. In this theatrical moment, the care and hope in the husband contrasted with the gleeful disregard by the dying wife left me filled with the wonderment of life and its seemingly unknowable relationships.

Yet not all people who appear to the physician to be rapidly approaching the end of life die. Some of them continue against the odds and do survive.

Brought to the ER by paramedics and accompanied by his girlfriend, a young alcoholic man with a history of throwing up blood was in shock, which itself tends to take one's color away. The drama of his appearance was accentuated by his dark hair, long and moist, wet skin and fresh, dried dark blood about the corners of his mouth; darkness along the central line of his lips showed that the bleeding was fresh. Perhaps most remarkable was his paleness.

The whites of his eyes were, on close inspection, purely white, with no little red lines. Examination of his palms showed no dark line in the creases of the palm, showing that there was not sufficient blood present, and the nail beds were very, very pale, really no redness present. His blood pressure was very low and his heart rate very high. This young man was in deep shock with no blood left in his system.

When the numbers started to come back, I could not believe the hemoglobin level. This number, which represents the amount of blood-oxygen carrying capacity, was the lowest I had ever seen, and that represents lots of patients and lots of years. The number was less than one-quarter of what a normal person his age should have available for a normal life. I was amazed that he could still be alive, complaining and fighting us off.

I need to mention that he was highly drunk and extra difficult to manage. The blood-alcohol level was about four times the legal limit. A patient like this needs to have medicines and fluids, including blood products, placed directly into their veins. Our goal was to save him, and his goal was to prolong the high of being drunk.

However, when patients are so ill, it is a major effort to place an IV into the vein, and without an IV, treatment cannot be started. In this case, he required a special and somewhat dangerous procedure of starting an IV directly into the large veins of his neck, but he was thrashing around and fighting us off while a nurse with a large needle tried to poke him in the correct site. At times like this, it can be difficult to remember to do no harm.

It's imperative to not tear one of those veins or arteries that have such important jobs to do or poke into and collapse a lung, which would make things worse. With a practiced and deft move, I hit the moving target and started the lifesaving IV in his neck. I was able to tie it in place without him pulling it out so blood could enter him fast, at almost a gallon an hour.

Shortly, his shock receded, and his color improved dramatically past the deathly shade of pale. We rescued this young man previously on the verge of death.

"Excellent save," the ER team congratulated one another.

"Wow, was he circling the drain," said another.

"We pulled him out," someone exclaimed.

"Great save!" said someone else.

Other than some of the violent touchdown rituals of a winning football team, our group could not have been more expressive or pleased about this clinical result. The patient was handed off to the ICU. We had won this match, though at some level our joy was tempered by the knowledge of the repetitive nature of this disease.

Alcoholism, drug use, intravenous drug use, tobacco use and other addictive illnesses continue to be major utilizers of the ER. The debilitating nature of addiction commonly shifts that burden to the society at large because those who spend their money on dope, booze, butts, crack and meth usually cannot pay their medical bills.

## CHAPTER 5

# ACCIDENTS & CONSEQUENCES

When I was newly interested in the field of EM, I worked in an ER in Colorado Springs, Colorado. Things were simpler then; they were more rough and tumble and less filled with concerns. I did not know as much as I would later; that comes with experience. One early evening, a night watchman was brought into the ER after being involved in a small altercation with a teenager.

He had to run them off a construction project he was guarding, and in the process of fulfilling his duty, suffered a stab to the back. The injury was not a severe stab, but he wanted to get it checked out. He looked and felt fine, and I carefully examined his lower left back.

I even had him cough and carefully probed the wound just like they had taught me in medical school. It looked great, with no bleeding or bubbles, only a superficial wound that did not get into the lung and was nowhere near the kidney.

This was an easy case, but one of the important, unwritten ER rules is that if he couldn't walk, he couldn't go home.

It's such a simple rule that it is frequently overlooked and can lead to trouble. We got him up to walk, his knees buckled and he almost fainted.

"That's a little odd," I said to myself, "let's watch him some more."

We did, and when he didn't get up and walk, I thought that he may need some fluids and an IV. That's when things really started to go bad. He lost his color and puked, his blood pressure dropped out, and he started to sweat and hyperventilate. He was blowing up. The carefully coordinating systems of life were separating and would never be brought together again.

I called for a stat portable chest X-ray and a surgical consult. The stat film showed some shadow around the diaphragm, the bottom of the lung area just above the abdomen on the left, and the surgeon arrived promptly and took charge. He immediately recognized that the man was in hemorrhagic shock and began working on IV access.

We used a new technique that had begun in the early and mid-1970s, starting a central venous pressure line in his neck. The surgeon was up there poking a large needle into the patient's neck, attempting to find the exact location of the vein, but he was having difficulty and stopped before he did any harm. Simultaneously, I worked on the patient in the good old-fashioned style, a cut down on the opposite elbow that I had been taught at the county hospital.

The cut-down procedure is slow and not as elegant as compared to the slick insertion of a central line rapidly through the skin into the vein. Line it up, push and pull, and just like that you have the IV done. We didn't look up and just kept working.

With some perseverance, I was able to create a very good and very large line, and resuscitation was promptly started.

While this was going on, we reviewed the X-rays. The operating room (OR) was calling, and it was so urgent that I accompanied the surgeon and the patient into the OR to assist. This was quite unusual in that now the ER was left unattended.

The surgeon knew what he had to do and immediately opened the abdomen. There was no blood, nothing. I was amazed and dazed. What was going on? We had missed the location of the bleeding; it was in the chest. Neither of us had correctly interpreted the X-ray.

That little wound had not caused a collapsed lung or anything severe but had nicked one of the arteries that run beneath a rib, which had been spitting out blood until the patient went into shock and almost died. This was not unheard of but was uncommon.

After opening the chest, we could easily identify the site of the bleeding and control it. We saved that patient. I went and checked on him the next day after my shift was finally over and the surgeon had written a progress note on this critically ill patient. One brief note: "Doing well."

What a case! So much learning, perhaps too much learning for one night.

———————

I spent 30 years in a densely urban area of Southern California. Roads and freeways everywhere filled with traffic day and night, weekends and holidays. The only time it really slowed was during the Super Bowl. Many patients wisely avoid the ER bottleneck by waiting until Tuesday to see their physicians.

A small example of unforeseen consequences stemming from an event was represented by the gasoline shortage and the rationing of gas in the 1970s. Citizens tend to take for granted the ways that access to gasoline helps society run smoothly. When there is a shortage or even a pause in the easy flow of gas, then problems big and small occur.

My scope of practice is at the patient level. I am concerned about the small problems. I leave the larger problems to society as a whole and the politicians and pundits. Some cases, however, demonstrate the unintended societal disruptions even if considered minor by the experts. The following three cases stand out.

I took care of a man who suffered a heart attack when he tried to push his automobile after it ran out of gas. In another case, a patient had received severe burns when he and his friends were transferring gasoline from a container to a vehicle. Another event very closely related to the gas shortage was a severe assault caused by frustration and irritations associated with waiting in line.

Order and disorder and the organization of society are delicate, fragile and easily disrupted. The consequences are usually negative, particularly for those with the least ability to adapt to changes. Those with minimal resources and means of coping will suffer the most. Those three cases showed me that when resources are challenged, the thin veneer of society quickly erodes.

In the ER, there was an endless stream of minor automobile accident victims to be checked out. This was either before beginning the road to recovery or to a legal settlement that needed documentation. From a strictly medical standpoint, the latter was an unnecessary medical evaluation taking up time, effort and diligence. That is the way the personal injury industry works, as well as the expectations of patients and their families.

Rarely, there are unexpected, worrisome traumas like injury to the spleen or even less frequently, injury to the neck, which could mean a possible devastating cervical spine injury.

Yet much of our time was filled evaluating injuries from minor auto wrecks where people had minor injuries.

---

As an example, a young man was brought into the ER by the ambulance crew, naturally in a full-on state of precautions: strapped to a backboard with an immobilizing cervical collar, arms tied to his sides with the trussed-up look of a turkey about to be cooked. Worried parents were at the bedside.

I hurried over and began my evaluation of the patient. I wanted to check him out, get him off the board and remove the cervical collar. The precautionary gear is uncomfortable, and no one likes to be uncomfortable.

The low probability event was not on their minds, so I hurried over and began to release the man from the board to which he was bound. I pressed, pushed and pulled with my hands, and asked if certain spots hurt or were sore. He was doing just great; nothing was bothering him. Great. Then I evaluated his neck.

Same basic procedure. "Does it hurt? Where? Let me touch it. There? OK."

I found some area of tenderness but not much, which indicated it was probably nothing. In another place and time, nothing further would be done, but in the US in the early part of the 21st century, almost everything needs to be done.

I carefully replaced the cervical collar that I had partially removed and mentioned to the patient that he should leave it in place until we got the X-rays of his neck just to be sure that everything was normal.

"OK?" I asked.

"OK," he said. I left the bedside and went about my business.

Just a very short time later I saw this young man, not mentally impaired in any way by alcohol, drugs or mental illness, remove his cervical collar, sit up and twist his own neck. He had one hand on his chin and the other on the pole while twisting his neck to show his parents that it was just a little crick in his neck, nothing at all to be worried about, and that his own self-adjustment would make it better.

In reality, he was fine. Frustrated, I told him to put the collar back on. I reapplied it and strongly advised him not to remove it. He went to radiology, where the lack of pathology was documented and then the collar was removed.

The correct chain of the process was satisfied, and the patient and parents went home. No harm, no injury.

---

Believe it or not, one of the most upset and despairing patients I have ever taken care of was distraught not because of harm to his person but the damage to his automobile.

The patient, a man in his mid-to-late 40s, was brought into the ER after being involved in a minor automobile accident. He was somewhat injured or not at all but was upset and tearful. His despair was palpable. I noted he was tidy, with multiple pens in his shirt breast pocket protector. He looked like an engineer, the type more interested in things and their workings than people or emotions.

Self-contained and self-reliant, he was very sure of himself. His son was getting married that day and he had an important role in driving his son to and from his wedding. The vehicle was a very special one, a perfectly restored 1940s Ford Coupe.

For years, he had been working on this restoration, and now that it was complete and perfect, it would have the place of honor on this important day. When it was over, the loved object would be given to the couple as a unique and special wedding gift, a gift of true love and heartfelt specialness. The accident had ruined it, though, ruined it all!

The long-filling, dammed-up reservoir of emotions exploded in that minor accident and all the feelings came out. He was despondent, and the family and I were unable to console him.

The only thing that worked was psychopharmacology, one of the powerful tranquilizing drugs presented to him. That sense of loss he suffered on this special day was of an awful intensity, and I felt sorry for him. In a half hour or so, he left the ER feeling better and that was all that I could do for him.

---

As this next story will illustrate, I have seen enough cases involving automobiles to offer this life pro tip: turn on the heater before buying a used car, even in the summer to test for the smell of blood. They can clean the surface after a bleed but not deep down, and if the heater is turned on, the smell of blood would be apparent.

Alerted by a loud honking from the ambulance entrance, we rushed outside to see a man who had driven up into the ambulance entrance with his now half-conscious wife beside him in the passenger seat.

She was buckled in with her three-point seat belt, and the dashboard and inside of the windshield were covered with blood dripping down the glass, pooling on the dashboard and flowing down the heater vents. A gastrointestinal (GI, stomach) bleed into her stomach was so irritating that it had made her vomit.

The diagnosis was simple, and we are well rehearsed in treatment for such ailments. The whole time I was resuscitating this woman, which went easily, I kept thinking about the awful smell the buyer of that used car would notice when they turned on the heater in the winter to keep warm.

Warmth brings to mind the long and wonderful summers in Southern California. The days filled with sunlight and cool ocean breezes, the full and varied delights of living, all having their own ER stories to tell.

———

Life and literature are full of irony, intended and unintended. This story is one of unintended irony. Young love is strong and full and knows no bounds. If a declaration of love is not enough, there is the chance to show feelings for one another with something more permanent, like a tattoo.

This early summer evening was just wonderful. I was working in the ER as the sole physician when multiple victims from a very serious automobile accident were brought in.

A young woman named L. was seriously injured, including severe internal bleeding and perished despite my extreme measures to resuscitate her.

My next responsibility was to the living. The driver of the vehicle, her boyfriend, was next to be assisted. He was not seriously injured. It is not uncommon for only a single occupant to be hurt.

However, when I got to his bedside, I stared at him. I couldn't help it. The tattooed images on his forearms spelled out the most ironic and strange message. Curled around his right forearm was the saying "Born to Lose" and the left forearm spelled out his girlfriend's name, "L."

I looked at him and had instantly read "Born to Lose L." moments after I had just pronounced the death of L. in the adjacent treatment room.

The sad news overwhelmed him. He dissolved into tears and was then helped by his family, who had finally arrived.

---

Another summertime story that left an impression is a young man in his late 20s rollerblading in the quiet of the early evening in a new pair of inline skates. Tall and quite handsome, he was dressed in tight spandex and brought to the trauma center strapped to a board.

This patient was unconscious and unable to follow simple commands. His eyes did not have the right look in position or pupillary size, suggesting brain injury. There was a bloody wet bandage wrapped around his head with his face exposed, and blood seeping from the wound making a puddle on the backboard. There were no other injuries. We began the basic process of stabilization and support.

The paramedics related that the man was skating when he fell backward, struck his head on the curb edge and caved in the back of his skull. He was not wearing a helmet.

The CT scan showed an extensive fracture of the skull and a very significant brain injury. It was certain that he would not survive, and after receiving comfort and supportive care, he died a quick death in the ICU.

The skates were new; I checked them out. How much the new skates and his height (more momentum) contributed to his injury I do not know, but it was sufficient to kill him. It was another one of those trauma cases where a man was taken too soon due to a sports injury.

---

On a related topic, don't forget about motorcycles! Summer is the time for riding, riding fast, and under all conditions day and night including halfway intoxicated or not at all. The allure of the bike and the summer sun, the girls and the speed are too much.

I have found myself dreaming of what kind of bike I would get if I could get out of my head. Something like a Ninja, super shiny with giant wheels that's sleek and mega-fast, but I could never bring myself to buy one because I have seen too much.

A single injured male in his mid-20s to mid-30s with massive head, thorax, abdominal or combined injuries was brought in deeply unconscious by the paramedics. He was stabilized, sent to the ICU to either die in a few days of multisystem organ failure, or to rehab as a "Gomer" (a person in a vegetative state) and would be home in a week or so to be placed in a "vegetable garden" (a place that cares for people in a vegetative state). There is a lot of gallows humor in ER. It helps with the dark side of the profession.

On the other hand, in an "in and out" manner, this biker's particular trajectory was brilliant and complete. Perhaps he saw a beautiful girl, turned his head to stare at her, and smack, ended up here.

The biologic thrill of the hunt and chase are in a way subliminally satisfied with our longing for speed. The high or the velocity both stimulate us and make us want more of the same. Fast cars and motorcycles are one way to get that ancient feeling of being more alive. As an example, I was involved in a case that I call, "How fast?"

A young man (it is always a young man) driving a Corvette convertible, a quintessential SoCal-type car, drove into a utility pole and was clocked by the police with a radar gun at 108 mph.

Accidents happen at any speed, but rarely do you have a sense of the true speed and thus the energy of the accident. All that energy must go somewhere, and the part transferred to the patient is important to what type of injuries they sustain. The mechanism and vectors of the energy transferred to the patient determine the injuries, and thus the damage to the body. Knowing this and seeing firsthand the results of unwanted energy transfer was eye-opening in my early clinical years.

———————

My biggest takeaways are simple – do not speed and wear a seat belt. When car shopping, go with a big, heavy car with plenty of room away from the body for when the vehicle side, hood and top crush toward you. Go with more intrusion volume (the space that is crushed in a collision). Gotta love airbags, too.

In this case, the driver, who was alone, was violently ejected from the vehicle after impact and was brought to the trauma center, still conscious but with only mumbling speech.

He was mumbling rapidly, going into a hemorrhagic shock of such degree that he would never recover. He had become what was called a "Slinky" – a patient with multiple breaks on a single bone and with multiple bones broken. He had left both his lower legs, including his feet and ankles, behind as he flew out of his sports car. He died despite our best efforts.

As quickly as it had come, abruptly, the summer was over.

# CHAPTER 6

# COPS & CRIMINALS

The modern county hospital is a surprisingly super-stitious place. As an example, there is no bed in the ER numbered 13. The ordering goes from 12 to 14. It is good business not to have a patient decline treatment because of a wrongly numbered bed.

The LAC-USCMC hospital has a jail ward, and that ward is on the 13th floor, perpetuating the idea that 13 is unlucky. The patients cared for on the jail ward are some-thing else.

Beyond the usual illness and complexity of human existence, these men are criminals. However, they know the importance of medical and social power, and they were always extremely respectful of me. The usual trust-ing relationship between physician and patient was not present here. In fact, they were usually trying to manipu-late me, ceaselessly working some angle or another.

The women were very similar in their manipulative behavior, charming, flirtatious and sometimes offering up their private wares. I've had patients look into my eyes and tell me how handsome I was, how I was the only one to help them with their pain. My tip for this situation is to be sure to keep ego boundaries separate and not be manipulated.

Prisoner escape was a constant concern, and staff members entering and leaving were carefully monitored on the 13th floor. During my time on the jail-ward service, there were no escapes. This diligence extended to the prisoners when they were moved to other wards due to the severity of their illness.

The county sheriffs who ran the transfer had it wired, and they ran it their way.

They would interview a drunk or weak-minded prisoner and make a comment about his mother. The poor man would always say something. The cops would tell him to be quiet and not to worry about his mother, which would set the person off again. Now the cops would have some form of resistance, and it would be their excuse to jump up and put him into a more secure form of restraint.

This was a form of fun for them, another moment to exercise their power. I was always telling them to stop, be gentle and to limit force. I did not want anyone getting hurt. It would only contribute to my already too heavy workload.

Routinely, prisoners were chained to their beds on the medical and surgical services and sometimes the level of security was quite ridiculous. There would be a gravely ill, traumatized prisoner in the surgical ICU who had multiple lower extremity fractures, in traction, on a ventilator and unconscious, with the obligatory chain on his ankle. The staff got a kick out of that thorough practice.

Though, let it be noted that the nursing staff applied a thin layer of gauze bandage beneath the chain to keep the skin from chafing.

"The harpies of the shore shall pluck the eagle of the sea." This line of poetry from Oliver Wendell Holmes represented feelings inspired by the immensely dingy and rundown L.A. County hospital on the chronic tuberculosis ward of the chronic disease hospital during my own dark night shift duties.

The patients were worn so thin but still able to live in tiny cell-like dormitory rooms so they could receive medicine from the state's nurses. They would regain their freedom after the court-ordered treatment showed they were no longer contagious.

Most of these patients were there because they did not have the resources or responsibility to take the medications on their own. They were in effect prisoners of the state, required to take and to be observed taking their medicines until they were no longer shedding active germs of tuberculosis.

These folk, though they were not so ill, were a very sad lot of patients. Most were skinny, uneducated and dull. Chronic long-term custodial care was required of them to make sure their lethal germs did not spread any further.

Generally, there is nothing like night shift nurses at the end of the medical road.

The nursing staff, particularly on the night shift from 11:00 p.m. to 7:00 a.m., were, because of circumstances, self and otherwise, older, heavyset, divorced, smokers, depressed, cynical and less interested in their work.

I did not get along with them. We were on separate tracks. I would get called by the nursing staff for the mildest of things even though they knew how to work the system and appeared reasonable, with good judgment. It was unpleasant enough that the night seemed to go on and on even though the actual workload made it more of a sleeper than I had expected. Cough, shortness of breath, sleeplessness, rash, itch, sneezing, nightmares – almost anything was a reason to call. The threshold for medical intervention was very low. It seemed then that the effort to ration care was about as low as it could be found within the hospital setting.

There was a trapped-in feeling in treating these patients in their dark and narrow hallways and tiny hovels on the lower levels of a sprawling hospital campus. I hoped that my life would not end up as theirs appeared to have. Had they ever been young, beautiful, clever and social?

———————————

On a springtime Friday afternoon, there was an armed robbery at a local pie shop. The local police knew the assailant was a bad guy and had done them wrong. He took a desperate risk for not much money, but he probably did not expect that the robbery required much planning or that he had a high chance of being captured. Of course, he was wrong.

The local police department responded promptly – maybe the silent alarm was worth it after all – and with guns drawn. The excitement of an in-progress event had their adrenaline running high, and who could blame them? The chase began and soon shots were fired.

The first injured was one of their own, a fine young officer who took a round to the elbow joint of his dominant hand, which was a career-ending injury.

The chase continued and shortly the perp was shot, cornered and captured, though not necessarily in that order.

In any case, shortly, but not too shortly, possibly a deliberate delay on the part of the police, the paramedics brought the injured suspect to the ER for care. His presenting condition was grave. He was wet with blood, which is always a bad sign. They delivered him from the jail because the cops said that they did not know that he had been shot. Seeing the patient crumpled up, barely moaning and sticky with the now-coagulating blood, I wondered to myself how they could have missed the initial presentation of a bullet wound.

The patient received a vigorous resuscitation and, despite our strong efforts, was pronounced dead in the ER. I think what really happened was street justice. This felon with a previous record had hurt one of their own. The police, in their wisdom and power, had let him bleed out in a holding cell until he was nearly completely dead, then they transferred him to another social trash management unit, the ER, for the final disposition.

At the time, I thought that this was a special event but careful reading and analysis of newspaper accounts of police shootings let me believe that this is a method frequently employed by the police – when they see fit.

---

In no way is it a level playing field out there. The pell-mell, reckless disorder of urban life is concentrated, distilled and matured through the time machine of the ER. Thousands of lives are shared within the rooms of corridors of the ER through the briefest of encounters. Such was the occasion one late evening in the pleasant cool of spring.

There had been local gang activity in central Orange County for as long as I had been in practice there and would continue long after I left the area. Most of the time it was just the usual: minor assault, overdose, stomping, minor gunshot wounds, the stuff of gangs as they created the action and necessary drama of their lives.

The quiet and drowsy feeling of an almost empty ER was suddenly interrupted by the doors banging open as two Hispanic gang members dragged in a fellow gang member for help. Immediate help. The aid givers, as usual, left before they could be questioned. They did not want to talk to anyone, not even healthcare workers or doctors. They dumped and ran.

They left their friend on an empty gurney, weak and bleeding. Almost simultaneously, but with a separation of 30 to 45 seconds, the same scene repeated as another team dragged their injured gang member into the ER and dropped him on another empty gurney.

The ER was now in a quiet uproar, overwhelmed by the difficulty of managing two severely injured gunshot victims. The diagnosis of gunshot wounds was easy; just look beneath the bloody shirt for little entrance wounds, about the diameter of a pencil, more or less, depending on the caliber.

Resuscitation and management of these types of injuries are very matter of fact, and while they were being applied, I had the staff put a cardiac monitor on these two patients. I wanted to see if their hearts were still beating in their young bodies.

Promptly, the answer showed up on the cardiac monitor and the paper tape. There were no heartbeats. No weak, little or disorganized rhythms. They had no signs of life: no breathing, no pulse, no blood pressure, no cardiac electrical activity. They were both checked out.

Dead.

A double murder. Sad. Our medical work was done. It was easy for us to stop, and we were glad to stop. Their life journeys were over so quickly. The rest of the shift dragged on with the usual type of nonurgent cases, which was just fine for that evening. Everyone was in shock from such violence and senseless deaths.

The local police department stayed in the ER for the rest of the night and into the next day as a preemptive effort to avoid any retaliation by the opposing gangs. Some of the younger staff members had counseling to help them with the aftermath of the whole event, and they reported nightmares for months afterward. I was glad to have the diagnostic power of the electrocardiogram, prior to the bedside ultrasound, which easily allowed a precise diagnosis.

Cases like this demand endless feelings, comments and editorializing among staff. Reliving these cases can take a lot out of the ER staff, and they have taken a lot out of me. They take too much strength, and, after seeing too many of these cases, I had no strength to give anymore.

―――――――――――

Around Christmastime one year, the government, in an act of kindness, offered early parole to a convicted felon. The intention of this act of generosity was virtuous. He was able to join his two other brothers for a family Christmas reunion.

There must have been some get-together. We didn't get all the details, but we could imagine the intense emotions at that gathering by the outcome.

All were brought to us. One dead, one dying and one gravely wounded. We put it together. There was an argument, and maybe some drinking but nothing crazy. One brother shot another with a handgun. The uninvolved brother took the weapon from the assailant, shot and mortally wounded him, then turned the gun around and shot himself in the head.

The first shooter just kept bleeding, and later died in the ER despite resuscitation. The murder/suicide patient had such a massive head wound that he could not be rescued and very shortly died in the ER as well. The initial victim was stabilized, taken to the OR and saved.

The entire scenario was over within eight or nine seconds, at the max 15. It is hard to imagine that kind of Christmas day for any of the remaining family.

———————

The east and west side of the great city of Los Angeles are worlds apart, and it is easy to end up on the wrong side of town. I was shown the great differences of that physical and cultural distance with a single word.

I talked with an upscale Westside woman who complained, not without merit, of difficulty finding a parking spot. She was "hassled" by finding a place to park her car, and who could blame her? Life is tough on the fancy side of town.

A short time later, on the Eastside, a patient I was taking care of on the general surgery service, specifically the 24-hour rotation that went from 7:00 a.m. to 7:00 a.m. Saturday to Sunday, used the same choice of words. Only his complaint was, "Doc, I was 'hassled' by a shotgun."

His liver, gallbladder and some other important stuff up there were blown away by a 12-gauge shotgun from a relatively close range, and there was still debris from the bullet in the wound. I took care of him for the rest of my time on that service and we got along just fine.

About a year later, while walking down the great central corridor of the county hospital, I heard someone call out in greeting, "Hey, Doc!"

I turned to see my former patient, once in the bloom of youth, still alive. He had lost about 60 pounds, still had tubes dangling from his body but was doing great.

Soon that "hassled" episode would be behind him, only a few more surgeries to suffer through and tubes to be removed. I hoped that his gang days were over, and he could have an easier, less violent life.

## CHAPTER 7

# "ALL THAT WHEEZES IS NOT ASTHMA"

Allergic reactions are common in the ER, so common that their potential to kill is not in the immediate thoughts of the treating physician. Rarely is an allergic reaction deadly. They are in the category of minor medical problems like a common cold, only a little bit worse.

———————

One patient came in with difficulty breathing. She said she had had a bad allergic reaction before and thought that was what this was. One look at her, and I knew she was right. Her lips were swollen to twice the normal size, and there was some swelling of her tongue, too.

Treatment with the usual assortment of drugs helped some but not enough, and a little while later her tongue was more swollen. A short time later, her tongue was so swollen it protruded out of her mouth like an obscene organ. It was so large that she was not able to move or control it. She had lost the ability to talk.

l had never seen such swelling. If she tilted her head backward the heavy tongue would fall into her airway, blocking it and cause death. Terrified, she was sitting upright on the gurney with her head down just a little. Gravity was on her side, allowing her to breathe a bit more easily but barely enough. l remained at her side, too, ready to cut a surgical airway or to mechanically pull that great gaping tongue forward and away from her airway.

After some time, the severe swelling went down, and the crisis passed. This patient had hereditary angioedema (HAE), a rare allergic-type condition. It almost killed her that day. It is difficult to identify the trigger for such events and what treatment will work to prevent it the next time. l wanted to say, "Don't let it happen again!" but that was just plain silly.

Other patients who present with seemingly ordinary cases of allergies, asthma or breathing problems may actually, and uncommonly, be moments from their death.

Shortness of breath, clots and a wheeze scream something worrisome to an ER physician.

---

Another time, the ER was quiet when an overweight, unkempt young woman came in for a visit, concerned about a wheeze in both sides of her chest. Her complaint was some shortness of breath but nothing too bad. She had a history of cigarette smoking. To me, this was a no-brainer. She was likely having a spasm of her airway tubes due to asthma. *Easy*, l thought. *Give her the usual treatment and get on to the next case.*

Not so fast. The history l received from the patient was important and changed the course of the case. She mentioned that, yes, she had had shortness of breath previously, and her doctors thought she had some "clot" problem or something like that. I didn't know who had the real information or where her medical records were located, but the case was entirely in my hands now and needed to be further diagnosed.

A concern about a blood clot jumped to the top of the list. A pulmonary embolism is a condition where a blood clot lodges in the lungs and blocks the flow of blood into the lungs, causing difficulty with oxygenating the blood. This can lead to a prompt death.

Diagnosis requires various imaging and the best one, in this case, was a CT scan. I thought that if she did have a pulmonary embolism, I should begin treatment immediately and not wait for the results. I consulted with the pharmacist to determine the correct dosage of medicine for her because her weight was a concern, and I wanted to be sure she was correctly dosed. Once the correct amount was established, I gave it to her.

This medicine would not make her breathe easier but would prevent further growth and development of the possible blood clot that I suspected was lodged in her lungs. I gave her inhaled bronchodilators for the shortness of breath.

At this point, she was breathing a little bit better, and treatment was underway for the potentially lethal pulmonary embolism condition as well. She was stable enough to go to the radiology suite for the diagnostic CT scan.

Off she went, and soon enough came back to the ER. We waited only a short time for the films and the results to appear. We didn't really need a radiologist for this one; the results were not subtle.

The imaging picture told the whole story: a large blood clot was within her lungs, waiting to grow or dislodge and kill the patient. We called ICU and made arrangements to transfer her there for further care. I told the patient the diagnosis and not to strain, cough or move, that treatment had been started and that she would do well.

She smiled and said, "I know all that."

Queen of denial? In any case, I kept up with her clinical course. She was in the ICU for some days, and with continued treatment, the clot dissolved and she improved. Then it was on to the hematologist to find out the cause of her recurrent blood clots and more treatment. The point, in this case, was the image of the large and potentially fatal blockage before my eyes waiting to kill the patient suddenly. It confirmed my clinical judgment of a deadly condition requiring immediate care.

———————

I saw another seemingly ordinary case of asthma with a 20-something non-English-speaking man who presented with a wheeze. He was so short of breath that it was very difficult to get a history, and no caregiver was present.

We started the usual treatment, inhaled bronchodilators, and intravenous medicines, and he did improve. He remained in the ER while we started his work-up. When I was sure that he really was doing better, I transferred him to the medical ward to be under the care of another physician. He did well for a short time before respiratory failure developed and he perished.

As reconstructed later after the man's death, he had a waxing and waning course of treatment, then he almost immediately had a cardiac arrest. He required intubation until he went into cardiac arrest a few days later. Things quickly got even messier after his intubation.

Instead of the expected quiet flow of air through the endotracheal tube (used for intubation), there was blood.

Blood was mixing and coming out with the air. It eventually led to his death.

What happened?

During the intubation, which was done correctly, a piece of tissue dislodged, and blood started to flow from the now unanchored site, the beginning of the end. A review of the chart did not hold any clues, but the review of the chest X-ray told the tale.

Later, in the quiet of the radiology suite, just myself and the reading radiologist under the viewing lights lowered for best illumination, we saw it, easily.

A faint shadow showed the offending piece of tissue in an unexpected location. The pathologist had the last word. A microscopic analysis of the tissue showed it to be a rare type of tumor. This tumor was inside the airway, releasing chemicals that acted upon the airway, mimicking the effects of asthma, particularly the wheeze.

Asthma and shortness of breath did not kill the patient. It was the bleeding caused by the tumor being knocked off during the failed resuscitation attempt.

The lesson, again repeated in this case, is that "All that wheezes is not asthma." It was rare. I learned a lot from this one.

What does one do with this type of information? Is it best to store it away but try not to forget about it? How a physician acts on this information is a bit more problematic. A doctor cannot effectively practice always looking for or worrying about the rare cases and causes of common diseases.

Should all patients be subjected to the most intense evaluation for every ailment each time they go to see the doctor? And who would pay for such care? From a systems viewpoint, there are not enough facilities to do that many evaluations.

---

It was very late, and I was just going off my shift when one of my ER colleagues asked me to look at a puzzling case that had just come into the treatment room.

The patient was a scruffy, bone-thin guy who spoke garbled English that I could not understand.

There was a failure to communicate. The history was not meaningful, and the physical exam was difficult because he could not cooperate. This patient exemplifies the difficulty in diagnosing without enough information. The information gathered from the history was not helpful, but the failure to give a meaningful history in itself was a diagnostic clue. What was going on with his speech?

The physical exam did not help provide any new information and the laboratory and X-ray studies were pending. These types of cases remind me of doing a crossword puzzle by trying all the known words or by having some insight into the clue and then trying simple words.

Based on the combination of signs and symptoms, I struggled to diagnose him.

My thoughts turned to the primordial mist of early medical school, where I was sure I had learned about this.

A deep and difficult stirring in my head led me to come up with a differential diagnostic list of a few things this could be. I was desperate now because the patient was not doing any better and was being supported, medically speaking, with no real progress. Suddenly, an insight came to me that fit the crossword puzzle answer to all the clues he was presenting me with.

Botulism. A rare (about 150 cases per year in the US), germ-caused disease that results in weakness and paralysis and is sometimes fatal.

A classic physiologic disease. Any physician who appreciates a rare and subtle diagnosis would love to have that one added to their life list, and, later, confirming tests proved me correct. I loved the mystery and precision of correctly identifying a rare disease.

In other parts of the world, botulism would have been easily diagnosed by the practitioner because it is much more common, but in the urban areas of the United States, it is still a rare bird. What a physician sees is dependent upon what they know and vice versa.

Some rare cases are becoming more common. The failure to get routine vaccinations and the antivaxxer movement will lead to unfortunate results.

---

An adult male patient came in with a cough and a complaint of feeling weak and dizzy. He was in his 30s and accompanied by his wife and child. He did not speak English, so details about his history and the presentation were not easily obtained.

I speak some Spanish, and the more language skills the person has, the better my language skills are. This patient was no poet, and it was hard to know what was going on with him. The physical examination showed that all was normal in the areas that would be contributory to his complaint. Then, as I stepped back and was leaving the examination room, I saw it. Or rather heard it.

He had a cough.

And not just a single episode of cough but big, long ones that took his breath away and made him weak. So, that was what he was talking about, what the textbooks call "tussive syncope."

There is a schoolyard stunt where I would breathe in and out really fast for 20 breaths and then a friend would squeeze me really hard until I would faint or at least feel faint. The lucky ones might even go all the way out in a true syncopal episode.

Well, this was what in effect he was doing with his great spasms of cough. It was not doing him any good, but he could not stop it. I decided to hospitalize him for his safety and to make a specific diagnosis.

This decision was the right one. It turned out that he was an unvaccinated adult who had acquired whooping cough, perhaps from his child who had not been vaccinated and was a reservoir of pertussis, a type of bacteria acquired from other children. The possibility of pertussis as a diagnosis had crossed my mind, but at the time it was very uncommon. It was nowhere near number one or two on the list.

The hospital later expressed concern that I did not place him in a protective type of isolation room since there was a possibility of transmission of this disease. Fortunately, he was promptly started on antibiotic therapy, and there were no other cases. The patient himself did well and was sent home in just a few days. This was the late 1980s; in just a few years, this would become a much more likely diagnosis.

The pool of unvaccinated adults was rapidly getting larger, and the number of symptomatic people made the diagnosis much more common. In fact, I saw the same type of illness two or three more times in as many years. In the ER, we do not make public health policy, but we see the results of that policy on a daily basis.

---

Another puzzling case that reiterates the importance of a persistent and thorough history taking is of a woman who came to see me at the county hospital with a marital problem – her husband did not love her anymore.

Rather mechanically 1 asked, "Why? Why does your husband not love you anymore?"

The answer was quite revealing.

"1 am not being a good enough wife because 1 am not doing the housework as before, and, because of the poor condition of my house, my husband now no longer loves me."

"He doesn't love you because the house is now dirty?" 1 asked.

"Yes," she answered with a straight face.

"Well, why is the house so dirty?"

The house was dirty and ill cared for because she did not have the stamina to do the household chores.

This was not depression. Something was wrong with the engine that was required to do the physical work of cleaning. A medical rather than a psychiatric diagnostic challenge was upon us, rather easily answered in this case, as the patient had significant anemia that was quite apparent on physical examination.

The oxygen delivery to her cells was so low that they were unable to do what was expected of them. The cells were failing the organs, which were failing the entire organism, which was failing the patient's emotional life and now her marital life.

Unfortunately, these sad stories are very common in today's world of on-to-the-next relationships. People's cruelty to one another is a stock drama.

# CHAPTER 8

# CARING FOR
# CHILDREN

From an emotional standpoint, I still stress out over this case despite it being years in the past. Although it is one of many deeply implanted in my memory, it has the added stress of involving the life and death of a child. This case gave me PTSD.

I was working at a run-down ER in the poorer part of town on an evening shift. Most of the patients who came to this ER spoke English as a second language, vaccinations of the children were not all that common and the basic wage came from employment in the underground economy. Most people would not go there if they had a choice.

The doors banged open, and the paramedics stormed in with a very floppy and gray child – one who was very close to death. The history was sketchy. The child was ill, then suddenly became much worse and the paramedics were called. I went back to the basics of resuscitation and securing the airway.

In this case, I would immediately intubate the patient because of the severity of the illness. Like most everything else in the poorer part of town, the equipment was not as good as it should be, nor did it work optimally. The quality of light from the laryngoscope was dim, so I could not see as clearly as I would have liked into the larynx, making a sometimes difficult task even harder.

Also, the suction equipment was not working perfectly, so the visibility into the airway remained obscured with secretions and wetness. Using the appropriate tube for that age infant, I was unable to pass the tube through the glottic opening. The pulse oximeter was beeping, which meant worsening oxygenation, forecasting death.

I impatiently received and then used smaller and smaller tubes as they were passed to me by the respiratory therapist. I was on the verge of screaming, "Get me a doctor!" even though I was the doctor. I continued trying to intubate the airway. I grew seriously worried that I'd have to cut a surgical airway. That would be a hassle, to say the least.

Finally, with much effort and dumb luck, I pushed the end tracheal tube down deeply and in frustration pulled it back when it did not pass with the proper feel. Stuck on the end of the tube was a transparent hollow cone of plastic! I had been unable to see it due to equipment problems.

This small cone had been blocking the infant's airway and its removal solved the problem completely. The child's color returned to a normal pink and the child started to breathe on their own again.

Saved. The paramedics, who through long experience and cynicism never comment on the quality of care, were so moved by the scene that one clapped me on the back and said, "Good work, Doc." This was as much of a compliment as was ever proffered.

That deadly little piece of plastic was from the removable opening of a plastic syringe used to measure the liquid medicine for the child. The mom had not removed the cap from the syringe when she squirted the medicine into the child's mouth. The plastic shot in and lodged in the airway, almost killing the child. After the crisis was over, I literally slumped into a chair in a quieter corner of the ER and began a personal recovery.

I was toast for the rest of the shift; that was as close as I had come to losing a child. I also spoke to the mom in my rudimentary medical Spanish and told her the child would be fine. I did not have the skill or the strength for the details, which could be left for someone else in the healthcare system.

---

In a similar case at another ER, a child of about 10 or so was brought in by the paramedics after receiving the usual treatment for an allergic reaction. The girl was checked and was doing better. No big deal. Unknown to me, here was a history of peanut allergy that was underplayed by the parent at the bedside.

The child needed another straightforward treatment for her allergy attack. This was administered promptly by the respiratory therapist, and shortly, the senior experienced nurse who was at the bedside called me to look at the patient.

The patient looked good. I ordered some additional measures, as I have learned to do. After a small passage of time, I received the same call from the attending nurse. The tone of her voice told me more than the words themselves. With my evaluation, the child was not moving air in or out despite her extreme efforts, as the small airways had shut down.

The child was struggling with death now, and I feared shortly it would be over. Earnestly, and with great stress, I commanded the child be moved into the severe treatment room.

With the help of excellent tools and the best drugs, the trachea was intubated, and the people and the machines did their work to breathe for the child. The acute severe asphyxiating allergic reaction was under control. With more time and movement away from the wall we were about to crash into, the child would improve and do well again. Had this young girl not been brought to an ER and the initial treatment been the only treatment, she would have died. She came that close.

I never had the chance to speak to the parent who was at the bedside due to the chaos. The child's care was assumed by the pediatric specialists who had come to our aid as the terror cleared. I learned much from that case.

Any procedure involving a child takes more care and emotional resources than caring for an adult. For example, the words "spinal tap" lend terror to the parents of a child who needs that diagnostic procedure. The needle, with all its historic fears, is inserted into the spine of the child. The parents have a "who knows what will happen" attitude.

It has the worst reputation and is generally the most difficult procedure to get consent for from parents or guardians. In reality, it is a little more difficult than sampling blood from a child.

During the procedure, the child is restrained, and the area is cleaned and sterilized, the needle enters the vein or space, and the fluid is collected for analysis. From the practitioner's viewpoint, the most difficult part of the procedure is the patient restraint.

If the child can be held still, and I mean really still, not moving at all, then it is not so difficult to hit the target, but to hit a moving target is much more difficult. Old-school medicine had excellent ways of keeping one perfectly still. There are very powerful drugs that will paralyze a child such that they literally cannot move a muscle.

They worked great but were complicated to use and require the practitioner to breathe for the patient, creating another level of effort and complication. Not worth it. Today's medicine has much better pharmacology.

Now, how do you safely restrain the patient, a thrashing, screaming bundle of illness who needs a diagnosis?

Hold 'em still.

The nursing staff would do that while I would try to insert the needle. Over the years and after hundreds of procedures with many different nurses, there were two nurses who were the best in keeping the kids still, and they had very different styles of restraint.

One was a male nurse, bear-like in features and strength, with forearms like Popeye, knowledgeable, with an intensity that allowed him to do the job. He would grasp the child at the shoulders and thighs and hold that little one still with all his great strength so that sometimes his forearms would shake from the effort. The child held in his great grip could not move to any degree that would make the procedure more difficult.

The other was a female nurse. She was huge, tall and morbidly obese, and she also had knowledge and intensity. Her style was to hold the child in a more delicate grip and then flex forward onto the child with her bosom softly enveloping and completely immobilizing them.

I always worried a little, though, when she was helping me, that there was some risk of suffocation. We were both aware of it and paid particular attention to the child's breathing, and later, when the technology was developed, would place an oximeter device on the patient to monitor the oxygen level.

Both of these nurses would hold the child so still that in most cases I was able to insert the needle correctly on the first try and the procedure would be completed in just a minute or two. Their skill at holding would make any physician look good, and I always appreciated their efforts.

Another way to restrain children for a procedure was to place them in something we called a "papoose board," wide swaths of cloth with Velcro attached to a board. The cloth would be wrapped around the child and then held securely with the Velcro ends. The stiffness of the board added additional stability and immobility.

The whole child would be wrapped up except for the injured part, which would be free and unrestrained by the device but held firmly by an attendant. Later we added our own addition to the papoose board – a Superman cape. The child's arms would be placed inside a pillowcase. The child was then placed upon their back, the pillowcase preventing much arm movement, and the entire child and pillowcase were then placed inside the papoose. This turned out to be a very good method of securing a child for a procedure.

I always felt a bit bad telling the child to put their arms into Superman's cape. Their little faces always showed surprised disappointment at not being able to move very well rather than being able to fly more freely. I hoped that the small toy or gift at the end of the procedure would be enough to compensate for their small loss of innocence.

———

Back in the days when I was inexperienced and youthful, I stumbled into a situation that I thought required a spinal tap, but the accurate diagnosis would have been obvious with more experience. This case was presented in the late hours of darkness, when I was practicing in Colorado Springs.

A young couple brought their small child to the ER. They did not know what was wrong with the child, just that the child was not doing well and would not eat enough. A common presentation: caring parents who know almost nothing.

In young children, fever may cause a failure to eat and a failure to be active. With that kind of history, I figured that the child was quite ill with a fever that had gone so far as to take over the whole body, known as sepsis or blood poisoning.

That illness could account for the problem, except that there was no fever. The temperature was normal or even a little low. I also knew that sometimes a patient could be so sick with infection that they might not have a fever. In any case, this needed further diagnosis and treatment.

A spinal tap was indicated. With the help of nurses, I attempted and then succeeded in inserting the needle into the back at the correct location and the correct depth when suddenly, instead of the clear water-colored fluid I was expecting, it came back red and bloody. I was emotionally impacted by seeing blood and was concerned that I had hit the main artery – the aorta.

I was not as worried as I could have been because the needle was correctly sized for the smallness of the child. I had stumbled into a case of bleeding on the brain, not an infection. The child was promptly hospitalized, and the appropriate consultation was obtained.

Shaken baby syndrome is when the caregiver, in a rage, shakes the child, and its head whips back and forth, banging the brain against the inside of the skull with such force as to cause bleeding of the brain and its membranes. This is a form of child abuse.

The parents were not forthcoming about the history and I, fortunately, did not harm the child by my lack of knowledge. My shock of seeing rich, red blood come out of the spinal needle was disconcerting, and I still remember the stress that moment caused me as a newbie.

———————

Cases involving young patients sometimes made me think of my own children. A mother and her teenage daughter were referred to the ER by their pediatrician due to a little problem on the backside of the ear lobe.

The recently pierced ear had become infected and was now a talking point between the family members, somehow symbolic of the independence of the daughter and coming adulthood. It showed that she had not correctly handled the postoperative care in managing her own ears. Of course, from a serious medical approach, this usually is no big deal.

The back of the earring, now buried in a wad of infected material, had to be dug out and cleaned. However, it represented much more than that. I have seen and dealt with these cases before. In contrast, my daughter managed her pierced ear lobes perfectly well, with no problems or infections.

I went about cleaning and numbing the site, and when it was clean and fully numb, I used a poking tool called a hemostat to dig out the earring back from the swollen, pus-filled soft earlobe. I gave the back of the earring to the family on a clean 4x4 piece of gauze, to show that the back had been removed, and for saving and reusing.

I cautioned the patient against using the pierced earring for at least eight weeks, asked if they had any questions and then discharged them to follow-up care. The wounded earlobe would heal, the daughter would wear earrings, and eventually grow up and manage her own affairs. Even though this was a little case, I enjoyed these small moments of helping people along life's journey.

At the end of it all, as an emergency physician, we see the natural history of human beings. The raw and unfiltered up close and personal. Kindness, cruelty, love, hate, ambivalence, caring and disdain. Whatever is out there comes to your shop with their wants and needs.

Some life journeys take a different path and not every child grows up to be independent.

———————————

An elderly couple, small, weak and impoverished, presented to the ER with their adult son, who was mentally challenged.

Imagine being small and a bit frail, and having a son who is all muscle, filled with great strength. He was somewhat unstable, got agitated easily, and they knew that at some level he could be violent toward them and easily hurt them.

The son had some kind of minor medical condition like a common cold that needed care but could not give any history because of his intellectual disability and examining him felt impossible.

It would be a huge effort if I had to force him to do something that he did not want to do. I took his arm to measure his blood pressure; it was like steel, and he easily pulled it away when I tightened the blood pressure cuff to begin measuring the pressure.

*No use getting into a physical or chemical battle over this,* I thought, so I backed right off and estimated the pressure. The rest of the exam went more smoothly, and he was safely evaluated and released. The parents were thankful.

I kept thinking about the bonds of familial love and the potential for violence against them from their strong and unpredictable son whom they never thought of placing in a care facility. Such is the love and caring of parents to children.

Sometimes the cases are fun, even touching.

———————————

I remember two cases involving mothers and their sons that could not be more different.

In one case, a well-groomed mom brought her child into the ER right after school. She had not seen the child for nearly six hours or so and, as always, was just a little bit concerned about being away from him for so long.

During this time away, the child had a most uncommon development – his skin had turned a dull blue color – a complaint that was written on the nursing notes. I would always read these carefully prior to seeing the patient. Blue skin is unusual and usually worrisome in the ER. All sorts of things were rushing through my mind like a failure of the heart, lung and circulatory system. I also considered a failure of the blood to correctly distribute the oxygen upon the hemoglobin molecule.

Wrong. In medical school, we are taught that inspection is very powerful in figuring things out, so while I was taking the history, I carefully observed the child. The blueness was not around the tip of the nose or lips, and the ends of the fingertips were fine. The child did not look to be in any trouble, so the big organs like the heart and lungs were doing OK.

Just like doing a crossword puzzle when the word pops up with a sudden insight, I knew what I had to do to confirm the diagnosis, or as they say in *The New England Journal of Medicine*, a procedure was performed.

I reached for an alcohol swab, opened it up and, with care, applied the organic solvent to the skin of the child's forearm and rubbed.

To my delight, and the mother's embarrassment, the blue came away on the moist square of the applicator, leaving a pale swept area on the skin of the child.

Dye from an article of clothing had come off upon the child's skin during the school day. This was nothing at all to worry about. The mom shrugged, demonstrating an "I'd rather be safe than sorry gesture," and fled.

This other case was a stunner. It took me in directions I had not thought of before.

A stressed out, unkempt mom came to the ER in the midafternoon with her two teenage sons.

So far, nothing uncommon.

She began by offering a vague story about an uncertain medical problem. I could not make heads or tails of her presentation. After she had been speaking uninterrupted for a few minutes, the younger son blurted out, "My brother fucked my ass!"

He said that loudly and with emotion. It was heard clearly by all in the room.

Now I knew the reason for her presentation to the ER and her difficulty in explaining the situation. The complexity of the case zoomed from near zero to the level of obligatory reporting to Child Protective Services (CPS).

A bit more history was offered; the older brother punished the younger brother by sodomizing him. The reason for this assault was the tattletaling by the younger brother to the mom about the older brother's cigarette smoking.

The medical concerns were still unknown. A full physical exam was required on both sons. Top to bottom, inside and out.

I separately and privately interviewed the younger brother, and he offered the same history as before. I received permission to examine him and to do a rectal examination.

The exam was not painful, there was no blood and the sphincter tone was normal. The entire exam was fully normal.

He was excused to wait with his mother.

Again, separately and privately with permission, I interviewed and examined the older brother. Yes, he punished his sibling for ratting him out to mom about his cigarette smoking. I still had to do a full physical examination. The exam went smoothly and normally until I had to perform a rectal examination. At that time, he demurred, saying, "I didn't feel like wiping today."

I asserted my medical authority. He agreed and said, "OK."

Upon closer inspection, his gluteal folds (butt cheeks) were packed with stool. I asked this normal-appearing 16-year-old to clean himself off. The exam was normal.

Everyone has choices to make every day. Some are more difficult than others. All have different consequences. He thought about it, made a decision and went on with his day. He made his choice.

The police and social workers visited the ER and interviewed the family. They asked me if there were any particular medical needs. I told them no.

The family was allowed to go home intact, all three of them. They would be serviced later by CPS and psychiatry.

I was shocked by the particular choices the older brother had made. He had sodomized his brother, distinctly uncommon, but his choice not to wipe was the extraordinary part of this case for me.

The public is nothing if not full of surprises, street smarts and variety. It is a large and diverse population out there.

# CHAPTER 9

# KEEP THE ENGINE GOING

Would you rather die with your boots on or your boots off? That expression was the one often offered to the hero by the bad guys in old-fashioned Westerns. The hero would choose boots off and then reach into his boot for a gun or a knife and save himself.

I never really thought about what that meant until I had been working in the ER for some years and had seen people brought in during their final living moments.

Some of them were slowly dying at home or in nursing homes and did not have anything on their feet except for socks. Others had the clothing and shoes on of their last activity, and that told a story.

A classic and sad tale concerned a man in full and vigorous middle age wearing a tennis outfit, including tennis shoes being brought into the ER by paramedics. On a pleasant Sunday morning, this well-nourished man had been playing doubles with friends and collapsed. He was brought to the ER, and there was no way I could save him. His heart rhythm was too far gone to be restarted, even with all the drugs and electricity in the world.

As they say, he needed a sky consultancy and that was not forthcoming. I noted a single yellow tennis ball in his left front pocket. Perhaps he was on the second serve, I don't know. However, I like to imagine that he died with his boots on doing what he enjoyed with people he liked. He died quickly and with his sporting boots on, probably not a bad way to go all things considered.

Unfortunately, in the United States, heart disease takes out way too many people, and it takes out about half of them with almost no warning. It's common to feel a little faint and then fall over, never to awaken.

The small irregular feeling in the chest area is a fatal arrhythmia. There's no real warning, only the fall. It is not necessary to have any pain or discomfort with a cardiac arrest. It's an easy way out, no fuss, no muss. Sometimes these patients make it to the ER. They have some unusual feelings and seek medical care because they cannot make their own diagnosis. People either drive themselves to the ER with palpitations, or they just ignore it.

For the ER physician, sometimes these cases are easy to recognize and treat. Others are so difficult to figure out that they require a prolonged period of observation and testing to know if there is a problem or just an overly worried patient. Sometimes during this period of testing and observation, the problem will become clear. The patient will develop other signs or symptoms, from sweating to chest pain, and then it is a clear heart-related problem that can be addressed, diagnosed and treated.

Sometimes, not too often but often enough that you remember it, these patients will suddenly and without any warning suffer the onset of a fatal missed beating of their heart. They are fine one moment, and the next they are slumped over and not breathing, the cardiac monitor showing the fatal display lines of the soon-to-be dead.

These severe and fatal heart rhythm disturbances require prompt treatment to save the patient, and by prompt, I mean within 30-seconds to one minute. Longer than that and the whole system can go haywire. The patient can easily die, or, if there is a recovery, the recovery may be marred with brain damage.

I have been involved with these sudden and explosive missed beatings many times and the abruptness of the onset is always startling.

The good thing is that treatment is usually pretty simple – just apply a firm jolt of electricity across the chest, and the misbehaving heart will come back to its correct rhythm. The situation will stabilize, and things typically return to normal.

---

One time I was caring for the typical patient afflicted by these problems, an overweight, out-of-shape, middle-aged male who was doing just fine when he suddenly slumped out right in front of me and stopped breathing. The cardiac monitor showed the typical electrical footprint of impending death.

In the ER setting, all I needed to do was push a button and the good old electricity flows across the chest and heart, correcting this problem.

The patient awakened and all was right and happy – until it happened again. The huge contraction of the muscles in the chest, back and arms when the saving jolt is applied hurts a lot, and no one likes it because it causes soreness later on.

This patient went unconscious, and the fatal rhythm showed no sign of stopping, so I shocked him. Wonderfully, the rhythm changed to a good and safe one. He promptly regained consciousness and then admonished me, "Doc, I don't know what you did, but don't do it again."

It was great to hear him speak and say that command. I made no promises but smiled to myself and thought how wonderful it was to be alive.

Not every effort has a successful outcome. One patient worsened suddenly and abruptly, had a cardiac arrest and swelled up during the final moments of his life.

The first responders on the team had difficulty managing the airway and tried to intubate the patient in order to push air into the lungs and allow the now-oxygenated air to be circulated.

However, something had gone wrong during the procedure and a little injury to the air tube was present, so that air not only went into the lungs but into the surrounding tissue. Each time a puff of air was given through the endotracheal tube, some of the air leaked out.

At first, this only impaired the efficiency, but over a few minutes of time, this extra air was misplaced throughout the subcutaneous skin of the body, and I felt it crackling beneath my fingertips. Soon it was everywhere, and the volume of this trapped air was increasing with every breath.

Instead of being able to push firmly upon the sternum, it was the equivalent of pushing against a sponge of growing thickness. Cardiac compressions were becoming less and less effective. There was nothing to be done. It was impossible to let the air out so the compressions could be more useful.

At the time the decision to stop the compression was made, the patient had the appearance of someone who had been hooked up to an air compressor and filled with air. The body appeared to be about twice its normal size, including the face. The features were like someone in a special effects fat suit. This resuscitation was not successful, though it might have been if this dreaded complication had not gotten in the way.

All substances of the body need to be correctly contained within their proper space. Blood, eyeball juices, urine, bile, brain fluid, joint fluid, ear fluid, saliva, milk, semen and even air. They all need to be correctly corralled up and not allowed to get out of the correct evolutionary space, or bad things can happen.

The heart, a fist-sized organ located centrally within the chest cavity with cultural and physiologic importance, is the cause and concern of many ER cases. There are plenty of cardiology cases in the ER, from a heart that is beating too quickly to one that is beating too slowly or even stopped, to another that is too large or too small for the body, to one that is working too hard or not sufficiently, to yet another that is "broken" by love or depression or stress.

To be sure, it is easier to keep a failing engine going than to try and restart an engine once it has stopped. Even though this analogy is not fully correct, it helps explain the efforts to keep someone going before there is full heart and lung stoppage.

These ideas were flashing through my head as I began the initial efforts to resuscitate another patient. We were far away from the center of the ER where the better-equipped care rooms were located. The curtain was drawn for privacy.

As we were working on the patient, his monitor started to show a slower and slower cardiac rhythm. The beeps slowed down and the time between them lengthened. It would not be long before he flatlined, with no beeps at all.

That same rhythm can also be caused by a simple fainting spell, but, in this case, there was no mistaking the overall clinical situation. This was a dying person, not some weak-kneed neurasthenic faint.

Assisting me was one of our best nurses, named D., who had been working in the ER for years and was an excellent clinician with great judgment. Whenever she said something about a patient's condition, I listened, paid attention and then promptly acted.

She had noticed the clinical condition of the patient and with dark humor said that the diagnosis of the collapse was just a "little faint." She knew that I would immediately address her concerns and in ER code was saying, "Hey, Doc, go do your thing!"

I was too involved and too serious to get it at first but after I had intubated the patient, now supplying him with more and better oxygen to breathe, and the beeps started to increase in frequency, his heart rate increased and the monitor sounded more like a normal heart, I got it.

Yes, this was ER banter. She had been teasing me by saying it was a "little faint" and now I could smile and tell her that she was tongue-in-cheek right, it was a "real good call."

Our interventions had pushed the patient back from the brink of death and onto safer ground, which is always a good thing. Had the beeps stopped, I was not at all sure we could have gotten them to start again. Who knows?

---

Something I do know – home projects can kill you. The DIY industry does not want the public to be thinking about those things when they set out to fix a house or repair an automobile.

Nevertheless, despite the hype and good intentions, the inevitable law of adverse consequences is always on the lookout for do-it-yourselfers.

One early Sunday morning project to get the automobile working did not turn out well for a younger Hispanic male.

With his droplight plugged in and his power tools scattered around him in the middle of his project, he was electrocuted. Upon the fatal cardiac rhythm caused by the electricity, he fell forward and into the engine compartment, where the electricity continued to flow through him.

He was brought to the ER quite obviously dead, with no signs of life and no need for resuscitation. His chest was charred and overcooked, with an accompanying dense leathery look and the smell of a burnt pot roast.

———————

Another lesson I have learned is that you can always add but cannot take away when giving medicines.

Early in my practice of EM, back when drugs were not as safe as they are now, I was caring for an elderly woman who was having trouble breathing from an asthma-like condition known as cardiac asthma.

At the time, we treated it with a drug that required care in dosing, but I was a new physician, so I looked up the dosage and gave her a full dose to help her as quickly as possible. Unfortunately, shortly after the administration of this drug, she went into cardiac arrest.

She was easily resuscitated, but I believed I knew the cause of this. I had given her a full dose of the drug, and despite the knowledge in the text, it had been too much for her.

This lesson was very powerful and took only a single trial for me to internalize. My style of practice after that grew a bit more cautious when it came to passing out any drug with serious side effects.

Errors can occur in the delivery of healthcare and frequently they are associated with the administration of medicines. The wrong drug, wrong dose, wrong patient, wrong interval. It goes on and on. Fault and blame are hard to place, and so much of it depends upon the point of view. Was it a local delivery problem by staff or a larger system problem necessitating a change in policy?

Was the person giving the drug under the influence of some sort of distraction? Was the illumination at the site adequate to read the label? Was the label easy to read and recognize? Was the delivery system foolproof?

I was involved in a case where a nurse administered the correct drug in the correct manner in the correct volume of medicine, but the dosage was 20 times the correct dose (i.e., the concentration of the drug was way too high).

The drug was lidocaine, which is a common one used many times daily in hospitals to control heart rhythm problems and as a local anesthetic. This time, however, when it was given in 20 times the correct amount, the patient abruptly had a grand mal seizure and went into cardiac arrest. That was quite a startling moment.

The combination of the seizure and the cardiac arrest immediately suggested to me that there was a medication error. Both of these serious side effects could be from that drug, while a heart-related problem would have only indicated the cardiac arrest.

The resuscitation went well and the patient survived. We determined the root cause of the problem – the packaging of the drug in the 20-times amount was the same as in the lower amount except for a small labeling change. This was a preventable error. It never happened again, but I lost some confidence in that nurse.

Another error of the same sort occurred when a patient received the wrong bottle of IV fluids. There was no change in outcome. Again, the labels looked very much alike and required too much visualization to identify the correct bottle. In this case, the worrisome bottles were kept next to the correct bottles.

I tried to have the nursing department move the location of the bottles but was unsuccessful. As the saying goes, the nurses rule the hospital and save the doctors, and the doctors save the patients.

Central to life, centered in the chest cavity, and foremost in the diagnostic and therapeutic mindset of the emergency physician, the heart has a very serious role in any ER case. Either as a well-behaved organ whose effort is taken for granted, or a worrisome one whose behavior must be ceaselessly monitored, observed and managed in order to have a successful outcome for the patient.

Cardiac cases can make the physician look like a hero if prompt control of a racing heart allows the patient to suddenly stabilize, or like a failed practitioner if a misbehaving heart leads to death despite the best interventions. I have been involved in both extremes, and again like so much in medicine, it keeps me humble and focused on the outcomes.

## CHAPTER 10

# "BLOOD ON THE BRAIN"

It was the early afternoon of Super Bowl Sunday, the day in America when the entire country pays homage to the power of sports and commercialism. A ragged, survivor of a physically tough life was one of the first thoughts I had upon seeing this patient.

This patient had sunburned brown skin, a short and squat stature, prominent silver dental caps, and well-used and hardened hands with dirt beneath his chipped fingernails.

His clothing was functional but dirty. He was wearing thick-soled work boots worn at the heels, and he was drunk, so drunk that he could only moan when asked questions in either English or Spanish.

Sometimes a patient like this might just be placed in the corner and observed till his drunkenness resolved. This "medical practice" used often by police for warehousing patients in drunk tanks leads to unexpected deaths each year.

We do not practice that sort of medicine. We knew enough that even though the patient appeared to be "only drunk," he actually needed a neural imaging study, or a CT scan of his head, to be sure that there was no pathology in the brain. The CT was ordered, and the patient was sent to X-ray for the scan. We waited for the results by the radiologists, which did not take a long time to come.

The CT of the brain showed that he had blood on the brain in a place where it did not belong – a subdural hematoma – a very serious condition that commonly needs neurosurgery. In this case, the amount of the blood was quite small, and it was prudent to observe rather than to operate immediately.

I went to inform the patient of his results, but he was nowhere to be found. After the X-ray, he had left the ER and walked away. He was well enough to leave on his own power and two feet.

This did not mean that he would not get worse. He needed further observation until his case was clear and there was certainty about his condition. The fault-finding, bickering and confusion among the staff started as soon as he was gone.

We called the local PD and alerted them to look for him, to go to his house, but the basic patient information was not available. He had been picked up on a street corner and brought to the ER under the name Juan Doe.

The efforts of staff and police to find the patient were unsuccessful. I imagine that he awoke the next day after the alcohol had worn off with a great throbbing hangover headache that lasted longer than usual because of the subdural hematoma but had eventually felt better.

Over the next few weeks, I expected some call from another hospital, the coroner or the police but nothing ever came of it and ER life went on. After this incident, the staff was required to undergo counseling sessions to remind them to adhere to policy, and to make sure that this sort of thing did not happen again. To the best of my knowledge, it never did.

This case could have been prevented by undressing the patient and taking his shoes away. He still might have gotten away but not far or for long. He would have been noticed by the public or the police if he was shoeless and in a hospital gown, which would have led to his recapture into the healthcare system.

---

Most patients don't associate a skin problem with something serious except to their vanity. I suspect that most dermatologists do not clearly inform their patients of the possible rapid and deadly aspect of serious skin cancer. So, the skin doctor cut off some little skin cancer. No biggie – except when it is.

It is one of the questions I learned to ask on the job.

"What kind of skin cancer was removed?"

Most patients do not know and that is probably OK, except when it makes a difference, like melanoma.

I had a patient with large scars on his nose and scalp from dermatological surgery who also had a known diagnosis of seizure disorder that was well controlled, although he had had two seizures in the past day. What kind of skin cancer? He did not know.

The CT scan of his brain was fortunate, no bleed in the brain, but he would require further neuroimaging to be more certain that his brain was normal. We needed additional evaluation, and it could safely be done outside of the ER.

A similar case was not so simple for another patient. A couple returned home from Las Vegas, tired from their three-day weekend. Those long weekends in Las Vegas were great. Stay up late, party and eat heartily. Sex, drugs, rock and roll, repeat. They had plenty of time to sleep when they got home.

The woman took a nap in the early afternoon, but she slept through dinner and did not get up for breakfast. A few hours later, the man was concerned enough and dragged her to the ER because he had never seen her sleep so much, even after "party time." Something was wrong.

Very quickly we ruled out the basics because the blood sugar was normal and the history did not suggest a preexisting cause. The next step was to push her through the diagnostic machines and see what they came up with. To make a diagnosis, we needed prompt imaging results from the CT machine and radiologic interpretation. We ordered the CT scan and the images crawled out of the video monitor. Now, something was wrong.

The CT of her brain showed not one but two areas of bleeding, which was very unusual, and it was the cause of her "sleepiness." We settled down to reinitiate the entire medical history. This time there was a clue that led to the diagnosis.

"Surgeries?"

"No," he said, "she had not had any surgeries."

However, on the second go-round, he did remember that she had some surgery on her skin, some kind of mole or skin cancer.

A skin cancer. Bingo. That was it. She had malignant melanoma, which could account for that uncommon pattern on the CT brain scan. The melanoma had spread to the brain via the blood and was growing.

We'd made the diagnosis and now the correct treatment could be started. Details of the patient's history that had initially been unimportant emerged as we went back and reinitiated the history process. The second questioning was very thorough and complete, leading us on the correct path to diagnosis.

# CHAPTER 11

# REVOLVING REGULARS & UNIQUE ENCOUNTERS

There was a patient we'd seen throughout the county for years. He was a young man in his late 20s, with a stocky build and heavy for his bones, sloppy and poorly groomed.

The story was that he had been adopted by a physician on the staff of the hospital and raised in his home until the age of 18 or so, when care for him became too much and he was told he needed to move out of the house by his family.

This was sort of a tough-love experiment in nature versus nurture. K. was different from the usual in his now-descended social status. He had been reared by folks who had gentleness and kindness about them.

When K. talked about his problems, there was a sense of friendship and equal social status, like he was talking to one of his dad's friends, and that shared position allowed him special privilege with the physicians. I always felt a friendliness toward this patient greater than the usual relationship.

The origins of his medical problems were obscure, but he had an array of difficult problems, including chronic pain, drug dependency, medical drug dependency, unemployment, depression, undereducation, loneliness, and a variety of minor problems ranging from fungus of the toenails to decaying and rotting teeth and early periodontal disease.

Somewhere along the line, he had surgery for his back pain (his adopted dad was a physician), and the lack of success of that surgery led to more back surgeries, beginning the cycle of chronic pain and medical drug dependency.

Despite a normal musculoskeletal and neurological examination, K. was frequently presenting to ERs all around the county following slips and falls. He would create a situation where he could intentionally slip and then fall, in a relatively safe manner, so he would be then eligible for emergency care and delivery to the ER by the paramedics.

Day or night, the paramedics would bring K. into the facility on a gurney with complaints of back, neck, extremity pain, pain, pain. We'd give him a pain shot and send him on his way. Buff and turf. This was the simplest practice of EM.

It was one way of keeping up with the flow of too many patients and K. was not really a patient, only a unit of care to be dealt with. The too-frequent visits went on for years, sometimes very often and sometimes less often, but they never stopped. He established quite a pattern. This sad-faced friend would look up from the gurney, greet me in a friendly and intimate manner, and the charade of care would begin again. I grew to like seeing K.

The best and strongest I ever saw K. was outside of the ER. I was visiting the county fair with my family.

He called me over, "Doctor, Doctor!"

K. was running a carnival ride. He had lost a little weight, was as well-groomed as ever, had animation and strength in his voice, and was standing upright without pain. He had a position of authority. He was the "man" in charge of the ride.

Charmingly and graciously, he took us aboard, showed us his ride and was particularly pleasant to my two young daughters. From then on, he would always ask about them whenever I saw him in the ER. He was doing great!

It did not last, however, and soon he was back to his old ways. A breakup with his girlfriend led to a downward spiral of ER care and the increasing frequency of visits. In fact, K. had the most ER visits in the entire county, a place with a population in the millions. Someone had to be first.

The county tried to put an end to this abuse by legal means, lawsuit, trial, a restraining order, etc., and it was successful for a while but not for too long. I heard that during a hearing, K. called the paramedics from the courtroom on his cell phone and was gurneyed away for more healthcare. He was a charming, friendly, incorrigible, sad sack of a case.

---

After talking again with an old friend who used to work in the ER with me, I was reminded about another great character who used to visit the ER all too often – J.

J. was more of a swallow than a wolf, a somewhat silly and foolish, easily distractible and annoying man who was more of a nuisance than a threat.

J. was a creepy guy who looked like he had stepped out of a horror film. He was too thin, had poor dental care, with a leering look and bad acne scars on his cheeks. He always gave me the feeling that something was going on behind my back.

He was in his late 20s to early 30s, unemployed and under-educated, more of a loner than anything else. Troll-like, he was unhygienic and smoked and drank beer to excess.

He was also homeless and his usual place to stay was under a bus stop kiosk. When things got to be too tough, he would seek a way out from his usual circumstances. That way out was cheap and reliable – get drunk on cheap beer, a six-pack would do it, and wander around town shouting lewd words. There was never any violence or destructive behavior, he just kept shouting his mantra of inappropriate words.

The cops all knew him and wisely took advantage of his drunken altered mental state to bring him to the ER for evaluation. For the cost of a six-pack of cheap beer, J. knew that once under the shelter of the healthcare system, he would have a safe place for the night, a change of scenery, female nurses to mildly pester and visually examine, a dry and clean gown to wear, and food to eat. A needle in the arm for a blood test or an IV was no big deal and well worth the pain and inconvenience.

He would be released in the ER to his "own recognizance" by the cops, evaluated by us and then let out in the morning. How many times was this repeated? Well, the social systems involved in this responsibility move slowly or almost not at all. J. knew that he could play this game for as long as he wanted, and he did so for years until he finally moved away. There could be thousands of people like J. in America.

---

S., as she was known to the personnel in the ER and the entire hospital, was an extraordinary patient. Her claim to fame was her repeated and prolonged admissions to the hospital.

While she was alive, S. had the greatest number of admissions and the biggest collection of medical records in the hospital's database. Her admissions numbered into the hundreds and her medical record was about 20 linear feet long. She was a professional patient, and, unfortunately, she had many diseases.

Everyone had a S. story. She grew up in average-to-poor circumstances in Southern California, was a high school graduate, held a driver's license, was single, unmarried and childless. Quite overweight but not morbidly obese, she did not smoke, drink or use drugs. Bright eyes, well-formed and well-nourished, she looked quite well but she had many problems, and behind her physical problems was an infantile type of psychosis.

She would not accept anything less than getting her way and getting her way completely. She would cry, scream, threaten the staff, threaten herself and do almost anything to get what she wanted, which worked most of the time. Over the years, the system institutionalized her, and she knew how to work it in her favor from each and every angle.

It was so much easier to give in to her demands than to try to fight her. In each case, her underlying physical problems would allow the staff to feel that they "would rather be safe than sorry" to give a justification for the admission. These patterns of behavior were well-honed, and the older and more experienced ER physician would always try to get the newer physicians to manage her.

It was interesting and somewhat enjoyable to figure out what tricks she would use to coerce the younger physicians to give her what she wanted. The system set the stage for her management. Her underlying medical problems were multiple and severe. Basically, she had trouble breathing and problems with phlegm.

She would get the equivalent of an asthma attack, bronchitis, pneumonia, even sepsis of such a severe degree that she would require admission and, frequently, intubation and placement on a respirator. This happened hundreds of times, literally. It is well documented.

S. did, however, have a trick of her own, which I was certain worsened her condition. Instead of clearing her throat of mucus, cough it up or even swallow it, she would let it collect and stagnate in her throat and airways. She made a very unusual sound with her airway, a kind of self-compressing snort that was her hallmark of airway distress. Amazingly, she would beg to be intubated and widely open her mouth like a hungry young bird begging for food.

Fortunately, she was a very easy intubation. With her well-positioned larynx and ability to open her mouth widely, this procedure was a snap. Once intubated, she would be treated in the now-usual manner and transferred into the ICU for a stay of days to weeks. She did not want to go home.

The social workers documented satisfactory home conditions, but that meant nothing to S. A normal case would go home inside of a week, but with her complexity and histrionics, it would take weeks to months to get her discharged. Once she even got to fly by air rescue ambulance to our hospital from a resort city in another state.

I could piece together the story from the transferring physician with whom I spoke directly and also from S. herself, who was still somewhat young at that time.

S. and her friends went to a river to party where S. got sick and was taken to the nearest ER by ambulance. At this ER, she went into her usual histrionics. She also wanted to go home.

Somehow, she was able to convince the attending physicians at the small ER that she required care at her usual hospital and these physicians decided that she was septic, and that the small hospital would not be able to care for her. They called me to accept the transfer.

Sepsis is a serious diagnosis and should be treated promptly; however, it can be treated at any hospital. It was clear that they wanted her out of there, and she wanted out of there, and the motto is "above all do no harm," so it's better to be safe than sorry. Thus, she was transferred to our hospital via a full-on air ambulance, which is exorbitantly expensive, being that the diagnosis was sepsis. She was admitted and treated for the mildest case of sepsis on record and then released.

We all took care of S. through the years. Her acceleration of aging was rapid, so rapid that it was hard to imagine how she looked before she became ill.

She once showed me her driver's license photo from when she was young and healthy. It was great to see how she looked before her many illnesses and so sad to see what had happened to her.

She had a polypharmacy of drugs she needed to take and was mostly compliant with the drug regimen. Some of the side effects were fierce. She needed to have both hips replaced and her body swelled up as well.

I think some of the drugs also altered her mental health. Amazingly, one of her inpatient attending physicians discovered that she had breast cancer and that started another whole category of disease to care for and treat. It was complications from that treatment that led to her final admission and her death.

Over the years, we forged a bond, and I began to see her as suffering and caring. After I learned of her death, I felt sad. We had gotten to know one another, and, underneath it all, she was a pleasant person who had suffered far more than any one person should, and now it was over. At least she was no longer in pain.

---

One case that recurs endlessly in the ER is the headache patient – chronic, benign and stable – an easy type of case if only they were wearing a sign telling of their diagnosis. When seen through the eyes of the ER physician, this type of patient is worrisome.

Could this be a new problem? Is it just the same-old headache? We worry we are missing an infection of the brain, bleeding in the brain or even a brain tumor.

Only with many years and many cases does the threshold for worry change. Eventually, it's obvious when not to worry. It's important to order more brain X-rays, like a computerized tomography (CT) scan or even a magnetic resonance imaging (MRI) of the brain to avoid missing something awful.

A woman about in her mid-30s was tormented and hobbled by her headaches; chronic migraines were her nemesis. Her name was Joy, and I could not believe the ironic discrepancy between her name and her issues.

I wanted to be wrong about what I already knew. Her well-meaning parents were wrong in giving her such a hopeful name, and there is sometimes too much irony in the world.

She was always coming to the ER for management of her migraines. I believe they were real headaches, and this was in the time before there were specific and excellent drugs for migraines. All we could do was manage them with an opioid injection. I saw her life evolving into one of chronic pain and misery from her headaches.

The medicine worked but left the patient stunned and a bit out of it. She was injected with the medicines so often that the nurses who administered the drugs would tell us that her buttocks were hard with scars.

Also, the threshold for doing a simple spinal tap goes way down. These folks who present with just enough worry or concern will get the little needle in the back. It sounds awful, but a lumbar puncture is very safe and a great way of providing necessary information.

This gives the physician the peace of mind that they have been thorough, and it is reassuring to have an exact diagnosis. Pain in other parts of the body is not as worrisome, usually, and the completeness of the evaluation can be deferred to a later or outpatient workup.

Dealing with the pain of these patients is still a test of judgment, experience and sometimes sleight of hand or mind to get them out of the ER in a better and more stable condition. Teams of healthcare professionals are required to care for these complex chronic pain patients correctly.

The one opportunity an ER physician gets to take care of these patients is usually not nearly enough. The patients with acute pain, the sudden stuff of accidents, kidney stones or childbirth, are usually easier and quite fun.

It is quite a cool thing to be able to take someone's pain away. The physician gives them the medicine, and they say when they are feeling better. Just like that, the drugs work and the pain is gone. It's easy to love that aspect of medicine.

I have cared for men and women in the writhing throes of sudden and severe pain from a kidney stone many times. Within minutes of taking a medication, they are so much better.

Such is the power of the physician armed with an IV and narcotics to take away the pain. A typical case might be a tough man of middle age, pale and sweaty with the pain of a blocked urinary passage from the usual kidney stone. In just a minute or two the IV is started and the narcotics are flowing into his system and his brain, shutting down the agony, and it works just like that.

---

One early evening, before the creatures of darkness rule the ER, a middle-aged male presented to the ER. Quite handsome with a well-formed and meticulous mustache, he was accompanied by a female companion who had delivered him to the ER after he suffered a stab wound to the left chest. I could tell that they were a bonded pair. As in so many of these cases, the immediate history was sketchy.

No one wanted to reveal what had happened. The details of the medical history were given up with some reluctance and my work began.

As I undressed the patient, more accurately "tore off his shirt" to see the location of the wound (because anatomy is destiny in these kinds of cases), I noticed that he had a spectacular tattoo on his right pectoral area. I quickly determined that the stab wound was not immediately life-threatening.

My attention was now drawn to the right-side tattoo, a very finely drawn and detailed outline of a female. It included the face and breasts, with shading and perspective. The tattoo artist had even correctly incorporated the patient's areola and nipple into the art.

I was intrigued. The detail of that tattoo was so good that I immediately recognized the woman who had brought the man to the ER. Yes, I had seen that face before. It was a great piece.

I had lots of questions and offered compliments on the design and placement. The patient by this time was not able to sit still and was going into shock. I had my work to do and did not try to get more details. I never did find out their relationship to one another.

---

I did get details on another patient in the county hospital sick enough that he was an inpatient, although I do not remember what his condition was or his outcome. What was so extraordinary were his ears. I had never seen ears like his before except like Spock's of *Star Trek* fame. They were pointed at the top.

He was an old man of Hispanic origin from the deep southwest. The sun had done its work over his lifetime, and his skin was dark and aged with multiple dark spots on his forehead and cheeks.

He told the story that long ago some bandits from the hills of Mexico, Pancho Villa's men, came down to terrorize and make an example of him. They trimmed his ears, as one would trim the ears of cattle, and then left that little dusty town. He healed but suffered for that cruel, crudely crafted maiming for the rest of his life.

---

Obesity can pose some challenges in the ER on a technical level. The personnel were not trained, and the equipment was not constructed to handle someone over 375 pounds back when I began practicing. Beginning in the mid-to-late 1980s, morbid obesity began to swell as a medical concern. Never have humans been so large. It's possible to be crushed or injured if someone of this size fall against a caretaker as they are helping them to the bathroom.

Moving them around the hospital for studies is in itself a serious problem. Doorways are not designed for such giant bodies and the portable equipment is not set up to handle them.

If one of these folks stops breathing or has a cardiac arrest, it is very difficult to manage them within the required time limits in order to save them. I always feel somewhat at a disadvantage when I am caring for the hyper-obese. If I had to go to court to defend the outcome, the tort system would not allow any special understanding of the immense and excessive difficulties in managing these patients. I believe the usual standard of care would be applied regardless of their size.

One patient was so large that the family brought her to the ER in the back of a pickup truck, a half-ton model. The story was not that unusual: she had been in her usual state of health until the family found out that she was now unable to walk and thought she would need medical assistance.

The patient was pleasant and in her late 30s with smooth skin. I estimated her weight at around 650 to 700 pounds. The hospital was not able to weigh her at the time of admission, and she could not walk.

Not even the patient could answer the question of when this disability had started. With the help of multiple workers from the engineering department, she was brought from the back of the truck and placed on two specially prepared gurneys. When we took her vital signs, we found that she had a fever, which was another dimension of illness to solve.

I wondered if the fever was related to disease or was from being exposed to so much sunlight on the way to the ER. There was no way her physiology could keep her body at a normal temperature.

She was admitted to the hospital, and our next goal was to identify the failure to walk. We ran imaging studies on her.

I thought to myself, "No problem, just run her through the CT scan, or do an MRI." Wrong. The lift systems for the imaging machines have a weight limit.

Calls were made to the zoological parks and the veterinary universities to see if they had the required facilities to do the studies. The nursing staff undressed and washed the patient. Fortunately, they found no bedsores. However, they did find an empty Twinkie wrapper left behind in a fat fold. Poignant. Every picture tells a story.

———————

A young female patient presented in the early morning hours with a complaint of back pain and some difficulty urinating, no big deal. This was most likely a urinary tract infection (UTI), maybe a kidney stone, or perhaps musculoskeletal back pain and urinary problems.

In any event, I was sure it would be an easy case, and I could get back to resting. The history was straightforward, and the physical exam was helpful. Examination of her back did not show any significant kidney pain or muscle pain. This was a good sign that it was most likely a simple urinary tract infection. I figured all that was needed would be a prescription and follow-up instructions.

However, as I viewed the skin of her back, I saw a shocking tattoo. In large letters in careful arcs starting from the shoulders and ending at the low back were the carefully written words, "I want you to rape me."

I was taken aback but kindly asked about her life and the circumstances behind the tattoo.

Her history was full of neglect and abuse. Raised by a single mom who was a sex worker and drug addict, with no male influences, she was a child who had largely raised herself. She said the words were from a song, but she could not offer any insight as to their particular meaning or why she chose them.

We talked a little more and then she was discharged. I imagined the surprise of her lovers as they viewed the tattoo for the first time. With dread, the thought crossed my mind that a coroner may see this tattoo soon, too. I feared that she was too wild to live very long, although I sensed kindness and goodness beneath her harsh exterior.

———————

The practice of medicine and particularly EM allows us to see all of mankind and its natural history. It's even possible to see the political and social forces of government and society at work if we look closely. The more basic forces of social evolution are there also.

Consider some of Darwin's ideas, the notion of survival of the species through survival of the organism. If the organism cannot survive, then the species cannot survive nor flourish. This principle was shown to me by a most unusual patient.

Imagine having a fully normal brain while being confined to a tiny, child-sized wheelchair powered by electricity.

My patient could still speak, had the ability to make facial expressions and some use of her arms and legs, but these extremities were so tiny that they could not support weight or do much else. I wondered how she could make it through the roughness of society when she had so little physical presence. This was the case of a fascinating patient in her early 30s with a rare metabolic disorder called osteogenesis imperfecta (OI).

This is a condition where the person's bones are so fragile, they will break easily. This patient wound up dwarfed and deformed by the structural failure. She was confined to a wheelchair, tiny, 45 pounds and physically very, very weak, just at the edge of not being able to function in society but still trying to make it.

Her power was in her personality. Before I cared for her in the endlessly busy and crowded ER, she had caught my eye and gave me a most pleasant look and smile. Her face showed great openness and acceptability. This feeling of warmth made me want to meet her. I felt friendly toward her. When her turn came and I finally did care for her as a patient, she was charming, had embracing eyes, a megawatt smile and a wonderful tone of voice.

In fact, she was the most pleasant and charming patient I have ever taken care of, and some would say that my reaction to her was a transference reaction or that she was at some level a sociopath. I do not know for sure; however, my reaction greatly aided her and improved her chances for survival. Her ability to produce sympathy in others was her survival mechanism.

Perhaps it was power; the kind of power displayed in infants and puppies and other defenseless beings, the power to have you protect them. I have cared for many other people who were very gracious over the years, but none were as convincing as she was.

The drug addicts were always charming and ingratiating with the stories of their needs but were somehow transparent in their insincerity.

Another similar patient was an older woman with completely crippling arthritis. She had been on steroids for years and dealt with all the complications of that drug. Her hands were useless for holding anything, they were so deformed. They were bent away from the thumb side of the hand at the knuckles to such an extent that a pinch with the thumb at the fingertip was not possible. The hand could not grasp anything. Her body was so frail and brittle that I was afraid she would break or blow away at any time.

However, she was mentally strong and accepting of her disease and condition in a very positive and powerful way. She represented an unsung hero out there in the world. She, too, through her helplessness, had developed special skills in dealing with people that made others want to care for her.

In any case, the regulars make up a disproportionate number of consumers for ER services. The curve is very nonlinear and more shaped like a bent exclamation point. The usage is steady in all areas of practice and geography.

Even the regular returnee to the ER may die of the known, new or undiagnosed illness. The history suggests, but does not predict, the illness or its outcome.

Healthcare providers, with a bias for cure and completion, get a bit frustrated by the returnees.

Viewed another way, these individuals can be seen as another way to make more money.

# CHAPTER 12

# TORMENTED BY THE DEVIL

"Pretty creepy" were the words my daughter L. used to describe her feelings about a patient I met early in my training, a paranoid psychotic, who had the words "love" and "hate" tattooed on the dorsal proximal phalanxes of each hand.

He was in a closed psychiatric facility. When he made fists, you could see the love and the hate expressed in the clenched knuckles. When I first met him, he was somewhat agitated, pounding one tightly closed fist into the open palm and alternating that pattern.

He had a run-in with the police, the details lost in the blur of time and the blur of patients. The county hospital had him fill out history and physical forms, including a rectal examination. I tested the stool for occult blood, as it was called for in the complete examination. I applied a small sample of stool to a paper and added a chemical that would show a color change if blood was present. The rectal examination can be perceived as threatening.

There is no way I would attempt to do something like that now after having more experience with the mentally ill. In any case, the stool was negative, and I survived that experience. His outcome is not known, as he was lost to follow-up. I also remember that I was alone in the examination room with him, and he was very muscular and fit. I could have been stomped or worse.

The paramedics brought in a patient strapped to a backboard, with heavy leather straps, wearing only the sheet provided by the healthcare system. His face and skin were filthy, hair oily and he was screaming so loudly that particles of spittle shot from his mouth. The screams were not of pain but of religious ecstasy as he exalted God and all the wonderment of the world and cosmos. He was screaming, "God is good! Jesus is Lord! Jesus is coming! Save me, Jesus!!!"

The screams were powerful both in content and volume and made everyone within earshot uncomfortable. Clearly, this man posed a management problem for the healthcare system.

The patient was now placed into a more private setting away from the public, and the ER evaluation began. It was pretty easy to determine that he was mentally ill, and once that was decided, he was able to start on a treatment program to quiet the "voices" in his head.

In this case, we gave an injection of strong medicine to control the wild mental agitation. "Vitamin H," haloperidol, is frequently used in the ER to maintain order on the mentally unstable patients who are having an episode. It works fast, doesn't have too many side effects and is safe enough for patients who are unable to give a medical history.

Within a few minutes, he was much quieter, and within a half hour, he was back to being a normal, unkempt citizen. I am in awe of these drugs.

Sometimes I consider society without this class of drugs. It's easy to imagine the ranting and raving of a medieval city with lots of people in the streets and fields making a scene. The chaos of the scene would be too much to allow the citizens to enjoy their daily bread with or without wine.

Again, the ER acts as a societal conduit; all the debris and worn fragments of the human condition are sent to us for management and disposal. The ER is similar to a gutter, where all the societal ills flow downward.

If a citizen has problems or thinks that they have problems, the ER is the place for them. Day or night, weekend or holiday, anyone can be seen by the healthcare establishment and a physician.

---

Rapidly pacing back and forth in the waiting room lobby, a patient was clearly agitated, and, soon enough, he shortly decided that he needed help. The problem was not getting better, and it was not going away.

With this level of agitation, we saw him quickly. The history did not match the physical examination. He was delusional.

He reported that he had been bitten by a rattlesnake and was concerned about the venom. He was uncertain when this happened and otherwise did not have any immediate concerns. He pointed to the site of the bite but there was no evidence of the skin being punctured by a fang, and no evidence of the insertion of venom into the skin and subcutaneous tissues. What was noted, however, were two, small, flat pigmented areas about a half-inch apart.

Like the kids say, "Duh." It was a freckle.

A few more questions and the diagnosis was cinched. The poor guy needed a referral to a psychiatric center for care.

However, before we could get him there, his agitation needed to be controlled with Vitamin H. The level of distress in this case called for a shot. Now, in a delusional man who was afraid of the already injected poison of venom, the delivery of another injection would call for some fast talking.

With the power vested in me by the State of California, a long white laboratory coat, a medical degree and a commanding presence, I was able to coax, suggest and command the administration of medicine that would reverse and neutralize the venom that was so disturbing to this patient.

The medicine went in and in less than half an hour he was calm, safe to be around and no longer a danger to himself or others. The world and the ER were safe again until the next time.

---

The mystery and delight of medical practice sometimes come from learning about the patients' lives, regardless of the urgency of the presentation.

This is a story from long ago before I entered EM full-time and had a part-time practice closer to the dark side of the City of Angels.

It was a simple type of medical practice with some basic infections, blood pressure control, minor anxiety disorders, the usual stuff that comes in all the time and everywhere. Minor dermatologic conditions are also common in general medical practice, and my practice proved to be of no exception.

Dry skin is generally thought not to be an interesting case because it is so common, and its treatment is hawked through the media. However, this case was so different. A somewhat obese woman in her mid-50s came to see me for her dry skin. She had tried the usual over-the-counter remedies, and they did not work.

"Doctor, do you have something stronger?"

"Well, yes, let me see," I said.

In the true and tried fashion of medicine, I started with the history and found myself quickly immersed in this patient's tale. It seemed that this nice lady was taking frequent hot baths multiple times a week and sometimes multiple times a day. How hot? I asked her.

"As hot as I can stand it, Doctor."

*Gee*, I thought to myself, *that sounds kind of uncomfortable.*

"Why are you taking such very hot baths?" I asked.

"The hot water drives the Devil out of me," she replied.

She said it with great conviction. With a few more questions, I found that this nice lady was delusional and had been for some time. She was stable and needed care, but in my judgment, did not need to be hospitalized. She trusted me and was willing to take medicine, so I started her on antipsychotic medicines and made an appointment to see her in a few days.

On the next visit, she was doing better, and her skin was less itchy. The pills were working, and the locally applied ointment was helping, too. We had an agreement, and I continued the treatment. After a week or so more, the Devil no longer needed to be driven from her body by the excessively hot water, her skin was not so dry, and she felt better about herself.

This was a great case. She continued to do well and came to see me on a regular basis until one time she did not show up for an appointment. She was now lost to follow-up.

This type of person does not often have a telephone, and she did not reply to a registered letter.

Shortly after she missed that appointment, I received a telephone call from one of the county emergency psychiatric teams letting me know of her whereabouts and asking for some history on this lady who once again was tormented by the Devil.

She had done so well that she had decided to stop taking her pills, and then had been reclaimed by her delusions. The psych team was not aware of the condition of her dry skin.

---

Here is another question to ponder. How much anger is too much? I do not know, but another patient I cared for exhibited so much anger and was so impulsive that it nearly cost him his life.

We had to surmise the details from what little we knew about the case. He was a younger man, in his 20s or early 30s (as is almost always the case in these stories), and was brought in by the paramedics, unconscious. The story, as presented by the first responder, was that in an argument with his girlfriend, he punched through a glass window. This is a common loss of impulse control among our society for many male patients.

That injury, as severe as it was, was not sufficient enough to calm the patient down. The rage continued, and he deceived himself so much that he tried to drive himself to the ER.

His nerves and muscles were pretty much intact, but the main artery in his arm was cut cleanly by a shard of glass. Instead of the muscles in the artery wall contracting in a way to preserve blood, the clean wound did not contract, and the artery kept on putting out many little squirts of blood. No effort at bandaging was undertaken.

Amazingly, first-aid as simple as applying pressure with a finger would have stopped that artery from continuing to bleed. The patient was not a Boy Scout. The little squirts after some relatively brief time caused the patient to weaken to the extent that he lost control of his motor vehicle. The speeding vehicle crashed into something solid, giving the patient a significant head injury.

The head injury and the blood loss were severe and created combined injuries that were very detrimental to the patient's health and life. Even though I didn't know how it got started, I had a very good idea of how it would end – in a long-term care facility, diapered and cared for by others for everything along the way.

This was another awful outcome I believe could have been prevented. The alcohol and toxicology screens, in this case, were negative and the outcome was most likely the result of a mood disorder.

———

Language is also powerful medicine. It can ease and begin the healing process on even the most concerning problems. Ask authors, journalists and poets about its power. Sometimes the simple act of asking someone to do something in a kind and measured voice is sufficient to ease a serious situation. It almost never hurts to ask, so give it a try first. It can be so simple.

Another lesson learned. A man named J. was brought to the ER by his caretakers. He was a late 20s to young 30s mentally challenged male living in a structured home environment otherwise known as a board and care. He worked in a safe environment and lived in a safe and secure home.

He generally did not have a lot of freedom, and he probably did not think about it much.

The caretakers brought him to the ER after he had accidentally overdosed on the over-the-counter pain medicine acetaminophen, otherwise known as Tylenol. No one knew how much he took, but it might have been enough to equal severe poisoning. We did the math based on the time of ingestion, amount of drug and his weight.

The chart told us that he needed to take the antidote N-acetylcysteine, an incredibly nasty liquid that tastes and smells like rotten eggs. I know because I tasted some in the name of my patients. It is truly at the limit of palatability.

It was necessary to get this vile liquid into the patient by mouth. These days they have an intravenously available form but not back then. We set about putting a nasogastric tube down through the nose and into the stomach through which we could pour the liquid.

Sometimes it's simple to insert the tube on a particular patient and almost impossible in others. J. turned out to be the latter. We tried and he fought us at every kink of the tube. We even gave him some sedation to aid in the task, but still, he was flailing wildly and unable to cooperate with us.

It was not a pretty sight, all of us ganging up on this innocent guy, wrestling him down, trying to save him from a possible bad outcome and always operating under the motto: *Above all, do no harm.*

We were exhausted and needed a break from the battle of the tube and needed time to rethink our plan. As we discussed what to do next, one of the nursing staff who had lots of practical experience with patients and kids suggested that we just ask him to drink it.

He was given a paper cup with a lid and a straw and was then asked to drink the medicine. The lid was to keep the fumes away. Left alone with his drink and some crayons, he politely did as asked and finished his required dose. He was observed in the ER, and after the requisite amount of time, discharged back to his care providers. We heard that he did well.

---

The things I've seen during my time in the trauma center have remained in my mind for many years now. They don't leave my mind easily and perhaps they never will. They have begun to open my eyes to the possibilities of events I do not want to imagine: mass shootings, bombings, riots and crowd-crush injuries.

They have changed me into a different person and perhaps a different type of person. I'm a little more cautious and worried about things than I would be without this job. I now avoid crowds and large gatherings of any sort. Too many people in one place will lead to some problem or another that I do not want to be around or involved in. Simple and quiet suit me better.

# CHAPTER 13

# THE FIREFIGHTERS WHO HELPED SAVE A PATIENT'S PENIS

The strangeness of medical practice in its entirety allows providers to see the range of the human condition.

A young man I was treating had heart failure based upon his weight. He was morbidly overweight, at 540 pounds, about three times what he should have weighed. This was an uncommonly high number back in the 1970s. We were all amazed by the size of this patient at the time, but 30-plus years later, as this country is in the midst of an epidemic of obesity, these cases are not uncommon.

I took a careful history and did a thorough physical examination of him. The pathological findings on the major organs were to be expected, but what amazed me were his genitals. The external genitalia had disappeared within a telescoping tube of fat. The external became hidden internally.

He said it had been years since he last saw his penis. He urinated sitting and had great difficulty keeping the area clean. Intercourse was impossible, as well as any direct genital contact.

I reassured him that all was normal as far as I could see and feel, and that it would return to a healthy state when he lost sufficient weight. He did improve while hospitalized and was lost to follow-up when I went off service after 28 days.

---

The world turned upside down, inside out or just plain weird is the everyday life of the catch-all ER. If it is odd, worrisome, infectious, bleeding or nasty, send the patient to the ER. Primary care providers know this and use that information regularly. Patients who have concerns about the proper or tidy presentation of an illness will also choose the ER to keep their privacy intact.

---

The heat in Southern California is plenty bad. All summer long, the citizens survive and flourish due to the benefits of air conditioning.

Behind the scenes, the workings of the system are maintained by the unseen professionals who keep it all going. Sometimes the machines break and sometimes the employees break. I was involved in a very rare and unusual case one hot mid-July when a refrigeration worker was injured by the very system he was trying to fix.

The basis of the system is the coolant that is kept within the system by tubes and valves. The physics of the workings of the coolant is simple – like sweat, when it evaporates it cools. While working on a cooling system, this male worker was amply sprayed by a stream of powerful coolant, which very rapidly did its job and cooled everything it came in contact with, including, in this case, his genitals. A stream of coolant hit him right at the zipper line and frostbit his nether region (private areas).

When this refrigeration technician presented for care hours later, he had suffered a full second-degree frostbite-type injury to his phallus. It was swollen two to three times the normal size, with large blisters on it. The rest of him was just fine.

He was hospitalized promptly and underwent the necessary debridement, cleaning by removal of perishable flesh and surgical management that would accompany such a severe injury. With amazement and irony, I was stunned by the juxtaposition of the intensity of the summer heat and this type of frostbite.

––––––––––

Medical school is long and postgraduate training may be even longer, but there is a reason for all that time in education and training. It is easy, too easy sometimes, to make an incorrect diagnosis in a timely manner. People frequently self-diagnose, or their friends and family attempt to diagnosis them, and too often practitioners working outside their area of comfort, i.e., dermatology doing cardiology, also do this.

The internet has the power to help and hinder the practice of medicine. Usually, it is for the better, with patients and physicians using the vast array of resources on the internet to assist in the diagnosis and treatment of common and uncommon disorders.

In fact, I would use medical sites to look up the treatment of even the more common disorders I treated in the ER. That way, I would have the up-to-the-minute ideas and understanding of the most recent treatment. This was better than a textbook, as good as the most recent journals but not as good as a consultation with a knowledgeable consultant.

The use and misuse of the internet comes to mind concerning a case involving a young man with priapism, a pathologically long-lasting erection. This may sound like a sexual delight, and, in fact, it is for the first hour or so, but longer than that and serious problems can develop.

During the erect state, blood oxygen levels drop, and the local tissues can begin to suffer the effects of lack of oxygen. Simply put, it is kind of like a tourniquet, and if applied too long, the limb can be lost. This resourceful young man spent perhaps 12 to 16 hours researching his diagnosis on the internet, or perhaps he presented to the ER after that amount of time.

In any case, he had his diagnosis down, and he was correct. The problem was in the delay in presentation to the ER. Prompt consultation with the urologist suggested that the long delay might have errantly affected the delicate regulatory vessels involved in the hemodynamics of erection. The elegance of his diagnosis was unraveled by the delay.

I felt sorry for him; it could have been something I would have done at a younger age. He seemed like a self-sufficient mountain man who did not need much help.

Sickle cell disease is another case where, despite prompt treatment, the results can be devastating. Fortunately, these cases are not all that common.

---

The heart knows what it wants, though sometimes it does not have a fairy-tale conclusion and ends up in the ER, again.

Polymorphous perversion is the ability of the human to focus sexuality upon almost anything animate or inanimate. A young man in his late 20s came to the ER one afternoon with a complaint of such delicacy that he did not want to discuss it with the leading up-front triage nurse.

The real nature of his complaint had to wait until he had the medical interview. When I went to see him, he was forthcoming about his problem. There was no getting around it, and the diagnosis was simple.

After inserting his phallus through a thick brass tube with a flange at each end, the distal end of his penis was now so swollen that it could not be pulled back through the tube. The organ was stuck inside the thick-walled pipe and the obstructing end could not be removed. Removal of the body or the tip of the penis would not be acceptable to the patient.

The technical problems were the thickness of the tubing, the depth and length of the cut needed to liberate the organ, the heat generated in cutting and the imperative need to keep the organ intact.

The goal was to not injure the organ in any way trying to save the man. Squeezing down the tip and pushing it through the tube with a little lube would just not cut it.

We called for backup: firefighters and the in-house maintenance department who would have the tools needed to assist in the removal. I always welcome another chance to use power tools! A small handheld electric saw with a new and sharp blade was selected.

The treatment room was filled with muscley men all inwardly moaning and guffawing at the awkwardness of this situation. The female nursing staff was displaced with surging testosterone levels of false bravado, and secretions of cold sweat as the men set to work.

The extraction process was relatively easy. The patient was fully awake and very cooperative. A metal guard was kept between the organ and the blade, and warm water was poured over the cutting site to keep everything cool.

With time and care, the thick brass metal tube was slit and separated, and the intact organ was liberated safely from the embrace of its once warm and lubricated womb.

Upon careful examination, the grossly swollen end required no further treatment since its blood supply was no longer blocked and would return to its normal state in a day. The patient looked radiant with relief.

He was given follow-up instructions, counseled regarding appropriate exploration and released into the city. We talked about that case for years after. Everyone knew that it was one of a kind and was pleased that it had a great outcome.

---

Another thing that is taught in medical school is the power of inspection or the knowledge to extract as much information from the situation just by looking at it. As it turns out, this information was extremely valuable.

After years in the ER, I was frequently able to identify problems and make a diagnosis with a quick once-over. As impressive as this seems, it is a skill that is also shared by the long-experienced personnel from the nurses to the clerks, though each had different perspectives and degrees of subtlety.

This type of diagnostic ability is particularly good when assisting non-English speaking patients and confused patients; in other words, those who cannot give a good history.

---

A man came into the ER just after breakfast complaining of the onset of sudden rectal pain. A no-brainer, as he was not sitting on the gurney with both cheeks, and he looked uncomfortable. Clearly, he had a hemorrhoid. I carefully placed my hands into new latex gloves, and with the proper gentleness, inserted a well-lubricated index finger into the patient's anus. When patients have hemorrhoids, it's extremely painful to have that area examined.

My well-educated finger did not feel the expected doughy sac of clotted blood but something unexpected. What was this? Suddenly, the case had my full attention.

I was not sure because something moved just a little, so I tried to remove it and was successful. To all of our amazement, I removed the source of the patient's problem: it was a fishbone!

And not a small one, either. This bone was about two inches long and extremely thin. Somehow, it had made its way down the entire intestinal tract and had lodged in the anus just prior to elimination. Impaled upon the terminal anus by its sharply pointed end, it was not released until I was able to liberate it and send it to my friends in pathology for identification and documentation.

The release of the bone completely resolved the patient's symptoms. Upon further history taking, I learned that the patient had enjoyed a hearty fish broth, drinking the entire contents of the cup in one gulp and swallowing the bone that certainly would have been too large to swallow in an ordinary manner.

---

Another surprise foreign body case was brought to the ER early one morning, about 3:10 a.m. It was a long time ago when ERs were not so busy, and I could get some sleep at those hours. I was awakened to see a patient who was about 16 years old and, still a little sleepy, I took the history.

His mother had brought him to the ER with an attack of abdominal pain. She was present during the evaluation and was worried about appendicitis. The routine questions did not disclose any particular worry, and I proceeded to the physical examination. At this point, I was thinking the problem might be constipation.

Constipation is a surprisingly common middle-of-the-night problem. The wee hours of the morning provoke anxiety that needs an answer, and no one wants to wait so they present to the ER for an immediate solution. The direct examination of the abdomen was perfectly normal. There was no pain or mass. The next step was a rectal examination.

For me, this was another ho-hum type of routine and, again, I gloved up and began the exam. Suddenly, I was now fully awake. Something was wrong – awfully wrong. I felt a hard mass, smooth and round. To evaluate it better, I had to push a little harder and the patient tried to squirm away.

"Be still," I said firmly as I held him down with the non-examining hand. With a sophisticated upside-down scissoring motion of my two longest fingers, I grasped and retrieved the foreign body I had just discovered.

To my amazement, the mother's disgusted astonishment and the patient's relief, I removed a seven-inch length of a carefully sawed-off broom handle. The mom was quietly freaking out and needed to be comforted.

The patient was resting quietly, embarrassed but quite relieved to be rid of the thing. I took the mom outside the examining room and told her about the "polymorphic perverse" aspects of human sexuality, urged her not to call her husband until the morning and to return promptly if her son had any more abdominal pain. They never returned.

―――――――――――

Another scenario, likely or unlikely, was told to me during the history portion of the medical evaluation by the patient. The patient was with his girlfriend watching *The Right Stuff*, a movie about the early explorations of space and the effects of microgravity.

They were fooling around, "wondering about how the astronauts would urinate while in space," and in the name of science decided to experiment upon themselves. They found a pencil-like wax rod. In probing the patient's urethra with it, the device somehow got "sucked" up into his bladder.

After a few days, he was concerned and presented to the ER for evaluation and repair. Fortunately, there was no emergency, and he was referred to urology for cystoscopy and removal.

The ER is the place for the removal of the great majority of the objects that get stuck inside of people or that people are impaled by.

―――――――――――

Another case involved a man who presented during daylight hours with a rectal foreign body. He said he was, "fooling around with my friend." The failure to disclose gender was the tip-off to his sexual preference. He was uncertain what was up there, and it had been there since last evening, but they were unable to retrieve it. A quick rectal exam identified a large, firm, smooth, probably plastic tubular object beyond easy grasp.

As you may not know, the human anus has a remarkable ability to dilate, to stretch open, very widely. With anesthesia, lubrication and dilation, most objects can be retrieved in the ER rather than the OR.

In this case, even with tricks of the trade, the object remained just beyond reach and retrieval despite multiple attempts. I then had the idea to sit the patient upright rather than continue trying in the lateral decubitus position, where the patient is on his side.

With the patient sitting upright, staring at my hand inside him, I was finally able to locate and retrieve the plastic canister.

As I delivered this "love" object through the rectum and into the light of day, the patient exclaimed with much enthusiasm, "Thank you so much, Doctor! I will bake you a cake."

I murmured, "thanks," and thought to myself, *that is one cake I do not want to eat.* The patient did well, and, of course, he did not return with any cake, homemade or not.

The foreign body problem in the ER is one of a simple solution: do not get intimately involved with any foreign object. It is foreign, separate it from the body. Do not keep it close or embrace it in any form, perhaps with the one exception of well-designed sex toys.

# CHAPTER 14

# OB ...
# OH, NO!

For emergencies, and I mean big-time emergencies, the obstetrician (OB) ward is the place to practice. As they say, disaster comes in twos and the OB ward provides huge problems and many opportunities for poor outcomes.

When there is a true emergency in the OB ward, there is a little window of opportunity to save lives and lots of chances to make a grave error for the mother and child. When I am called to assist in the OB ward, I shudder.

Most of the time it is an easy, straightforward delivery of a child just prior to the arrival of the OB physician. After sorting them out, these cases are usually somewhat enjoyable for everyone, since the delivery of a healthy baby is always exciting – although the nurses wish their usual doctor was there, and the patient who is just glad to have somebody there is usually slightly disappointed not to have her regular physician.

The main task is to get control of the head and smoothly deliver the baby. It is so easy that it can be done without medical care in most cases and in many parts of the world.

If more needs to be done, deliver the placenta and repair any vaginal lacerations. Easy and cool. I can usually be back at work in the ER inside of 15–30 minutes if all goes well.

———————

I was once called to OB for a cardiac arrest. This laboring patient went into cardiorespiratory arrest, stopped breathing, turned blue and lost her heartbeat. Following a prolonged and difficult resuscitation in the OB suite, she died a few days later in the ICU after a multiorgan system failure.

She had suffered a rare and not uncommonly fatal amniotic fluid embolus. The liquid surrounding the baby got blasted into her bloodstream and lungs, causing a complete shutdown. I have only seen two of these cases in my ER practice, which is more times than many full-time OBs.

Obviously, I flinch when I am called to the OB ward. The management of a floppy baby is worrisome. The babies are tough, I can almost always get them a heartbeat, to a respirator and to a neonatal ICU, but the legal exposure is great and daunting.

———————

C-sections are considered outside the scope of EM practice in the United States. Certainly, I have seen enough cases to do one, but that rudimentary skill would not stand up to the current tort system.

Once I was called to the labor and delivery (L&D) department to manage a difficult birth, with the fetal heart beats severely dropping. At the last instant, as I was pressing down on the skin with a new scalpel in my gloved hands, I was saved from doing a C-section by the arrival of the OB.

This was such a relief! I was relieved from the consequences of judgment, and I did not have to decide to proceed
or not to proceed. I even had the chance to hang out and
learn how the professionals carefully did the procedure.

———————

I have had other cases where the mother did not know she
was pregnant until just before delivery, and by just before
I mean into the second stage of labor when the head starts
to come out.

One case involved a healthy young woman who denied
her pregnancy by saying that she could not be pregnant
because she was able to carry a backpack for extended
trips into the High Sierra mountains.

Wrong. She was pregnant and delivered a perfectly
healthy infant.

———————

Generally, in my practice of medicine, I make it a point to
view all my patients with a kind and understanding outlook.

Complaining of abdominal cramps and pain without
diarrhea, a 15- to 16-year-old female presented to the ER
one morning. This was a nonserious case, so she was tri-
aged to the waiting room, while other more urgent cases
were seen, and she got up to use the restroom.

The staff heard loud painful groaning coming from
the restroom, but the teenager did not answer when they
called out to ask if she was all right. They eventually
opened the door and found this young girl squatting on
the rim of the toilet, a stretched, torn and bleeding umbil-
ical cord dangling from between her legs and a full-term
newborn on the cold tile floor.

Quickly, mother and child were brought to a treatment area where evaluation showed that the mother was doing just fine, and the placenta was delivered without difficulty. The newborn was not doing as well. The delivery was wickedly sudden and unfortunate, and the baby did not survive.

Intimacy in the practice of medicine comes in many forms, most often in a more joyless and heavy manner. Death is a big part of life and an even bigger part of the medical practice. Uncommonly, there is joy and hope in the practice of EM. It is welcome and appreciated and so rare that when it happens it is delightful.

---

I was caring for a young woman, no more than 12 or 13, for an abdominal complaint. This is always a difficult age to get an accurate and reliable history for any complaint between the ribs and the knees. Routinely, I would ask about a menstrual history, when was the onset of menarche and when was the last period.

This patient answered that she had never had a period, then added that she had recently delivered a baby. No, this was not some endocrinologic wonder, but the pathetic result of an abusive uncle who had been living with her for months. The patient became pregnant prior to the first endometrial sloughing, i.e., period.

It was hard for me to imagine her outlook on life, but easy to understand why she was not doing as well in school. This was another case that was unfortunately lost to follow-up.

---

In another abuse case, the patient could not give a history, and, in the early morning hours, it was all a bit of a blur.

Too many people were talking all at once without providing information to help us sort it all out.

The patient had severe Down syndrome, she could not speak and would only grunt and make other noises when she was irritated or stimulated. Her caretakers had brought her in because she had just delivered a baby. The baby was in a plastic sack, dead, but the mom was doing just fine. Her developmental disability removed her from understanding the circumstances of her situation.

There was no problem of a medical nature, and from the ER viewpoint, she would soon be stable enough to go to postpartum, as would any other uncomplicated delivery. Of course, the staff called the police, who responded to the ER in a flash, with visions of murder, rape, abuse and neglect at the top of their minds.

The horrors of this case made the newspapers and the news for a full two days. The father of the baby was the husband of the girl's caregiver, and the baby was stillborn. Thus, there was no need for a murder investigation. The mom was ready for discharge after a day.

Attorneys became involved in the case, and I was called to give a deposition about the rape. I was called because I was the first person to have primary knowledge of the case.

Interestingly, she had been seen in the ER during the unrecognized pregnancy for some sort of minor medical problem and had never been diagnosed with anything. I was asked to describe the case and to describe the mental state of the patient.

I then had the chance to make sounds to simulate the response of the patient to my questions during the physical examinations. I went on to describe the case as "creepy." This was a clear but less sophisticated term, and I think the plaintiff attorney liked it. It would make his case much stronger. The perp was convicted and sentenced to a long term.

Trauma cases, always alarming, can be uninteresting, desperate or anywhere in-between.

Emotionally, it is relatively easy to deal with ordinary accidents such as a common automobile accident where no one is seriously hurt. An auto accident when one driver has been drinking with minimal damage to the passengers takes it up another emotional notch, drinking with a serious injury is another escalation of emotional input and so it goes.

Incrementally, the pain and toll of illness create a hierarchy of traumatic stress for the providers and caregivers. The effects are gently cumulative. Some of the rare and deeply unfortunate trauma cases, ones that force deep medical and surgical concentration of effort and allow a glimpse into the staggering unsettled minds of the participants, are the cases that accelerate a caregiver's stress disorder.

---

I was involved in a case that bored its way deep into my mind, finally only put to rest by the birth of my first daughter.

This was a period when the hospital was a trauma center, and the ER received some of the most severely ill and most distressed patients. Their physical condition was just awful, and their chances of survival were tentative at best. In some of these cases, the psychological torment behind the patients and the patients' lives were equally severe. The passions of these lives could be hard to imagine.

The patient was an infant, I cannot remember if it was a boy or girl, but the baby was brought in by the paramedics during daylight hours. The precise detail of the events prior to admission were not available, as is often the case.

Prior to arrival at the ER, this innocent child was being held by one of the parents, shield like, when the child was stabbed in the back by the other parent. The stab wound created a "sucking chest wound," causing great respiratory distress that required immediate surgical repair, which was done promptly in the ER with excellent results. The improvement of the respiratory status was very gratifying.

The wound, however, was so close to the spine that it had cut into the spinal cord and the child suffered an injury to the nerves that controlled their legs – paraplegia would be the probable result. This disastrous result of the parents' thought processes was too shocking, raw, primitive and uncivilized to try and understand.

I could only do my job. The scene and emotions were so haunting that, though I tried to bury them, they wormed themselves into my mind and remained there until they were released by my daughter L.'s birth.

At the time of her birth, I was an older dad, and I was emotional, tearful and filled with very deep feelings than I had ever felt before. During this birthing period, I briefly remembered the case and rid myself of the burdensome quality that had persisted for years.

I do not know precisely what the release mechanism was or what caused it to surface after so many years. Perhaps it was the depth of feelings that I was experiencing, putting me on the level of the tiny patient's parents.

Only the intensity, depth and deeply held primitive sense of emotion were the same. We caregivers working on the stabbed infant all were looking at the event on the horizon of human emotions, over the edge and into the void. Often repeated, these kinds of cases lead me to feeling like I had seen too much.

The role of the ER in the management of the OB might, with some humor, be best described as a "place of last resort," "anywhere but here" and other phrases that attest to the separate criticality of the specialty.

Of course, the OB is seen and carefully cared for in the ER but really should be managed outside of the ER for the comfort and safety of the patient and baby. Other than the simplest cases – think the first trimester – the OB gives the ER practitioner an accelerating rate of stress and worry.

Any time I am called to the L&D suite, it is a worry. There are emergencies, then there are OB emergencies. These involve the severe crisis of a delivery going sideways or gone completely wrong, both for mother and baby.

# CHAPTER 15

# SUDDEN & UNEXPECTED

What do people think when they meet a real-life EM physician face to face? The popular TV shows about doctors and hospitals have created expectations of medical behaviors and the question becomes, "Does life mimic art or vice versa?" Almost everyone wants to know what the worst thing is that I have seen, done and experienced.

It is so hard to answer. Every practitioner has medical demons and occult fears that would make it to their "worst ever" list. Now, the worst cases may not come with violence or explosive force; sometimes they arrive with a dreadful prolonged ungentleness and disquieting feeling that can be haunting.

Emergency medicine requires balance and equanimity with all its ceaseless assaults on one's personal sanity, and an assault on what we hold sacred. So, it was not surprising to me after about 10 years of practice that I wanted to get to a place of calmness, control and beauty, a place with a more natural rhythm and harmony than in my work-a-day world.

To that end, my wife and I purchased a rural piece of property, a beat-up vineyard and unimproved house, both needing rehab, an end of the road kind of place in what was at the time a quiet agricultural town.

We slowly got the balance we wanted. It took a few years to get the rhythm of the seasons down. The day-to-day variations in weather and the variation of each annual seasonal change taught us observation and acceptance of the variables that we could not control. Similar to flying, which might be scary, but nothing can be done to change the outcome of a flight once on board.

Also, in a certain way, doesn't everyone want to be a cowboy?

We had the pleasure of growing a variety of crops and orchard harvests, and had dogs, chickens, cattle (Longhorns) and, of course, horses.

All of these added to the depth and richness of the rural experience, the good, the bad and the in-between, like when we had to put Lightning down, a wonderful 34-year-old mare who had suffered long enough with multiple medical problems.

Her arthritis was so severe that her hind legs could not be picked up for the person who shoes horses. She also had a mouth full of hard melanoma nodules that interfered with eating, a swayback with the appearance of a suspension bridge and a blinding eye condition – a deep corneal abrasion with severe conjunctivitis that would not heal despite multiple antibiotics. We had to sew the eye closed.

The eye did not heal, and we decided to put her down. It was difficult to know if we'd made the right decision.

---

Lightning's saga reminded me of a remarkable case I once dealt with. I was caring for a woman who was having some shortness of breath but no chest pain, which was rather routine. I noticed in examining her that she was blind, and not only blind but had no eyeballs present. Certainly, this was not a common surgical type of procedure.

I asked her to give some more history about her visual loss. She answered in a perfectly even tone of voice, completely matter of fact as though she might have been reading from last week's grocery list, "My son gouged my eyes out."

And that was that. A psychotic son in an act of biblical proportion had changed her life forever.

The flatness and blandness of the answer in contrast to the event were so striking. I was filled with questions and wanted to hear the whole story of her life with her son. However, her difficulty breathing was paramount, and I feared the trauma in retelling that story would have provoked her too much, so I kept the questions to myself.

Most people expect the ordinary world, where most people spend almost all their time, to be ordered and predictable, and for life to be mostly ordinary and mundane.

A daughter made a Christmas visit to her mom who was safely installed in a nursing home. The daughter, who lived out of town, visited whenever she could but not too often. Her mother was mostly bedridden and was sitting propped upright in a hospital bed, the kind that allows the head of the bed to be elevated. She had been nicely made up by the nursing home staff for the festive occasion: her hair, lips and nails were done.

The daughter, excitedly greeting her mom, lifted her up and forward by the upper arms, inadvertently breaking both of them. The daughter instantly noticed the crunch and deformity, and the mom was brought to medical attention promptly. The uncommon presentation of bilateral upper humerus fractures – upper arm breaks on both sides – made us initially suspect the possibility of elder abuse.

However, this was dismissed when X-rays showed that the fractures were from a pathologically weakened bone. The poor mom unknowingly had bone cancer, and the daughter was there at its presentation. Ugh!

Mom was admitted for further treatment. It's easy to imagine the way the daughter was feeling as she reviewed the day and her actions.

In the ER, the movement away from that ordinary is concentrated and distilled into one night or a few hours. It is a place where order is forced upon the unbending universal disorder.

The violent ones, the really violent ones, never make it to the ER. They are pronounced dead in the field and belong to the special interests of the police, fire department and military types. Bodies blown apart, squashed and destroyed are best appreciated at the coroner's office. There they can see the grim unsalvageable debris from the city.

Emergency rooms have more life in them, though sometimes it is quickly ebbing away. Many times, people come in talking and die right in front of us. I have never liked having someone come in talking and then die on me. Even my kids used to ask what was the worst thing I have seen. Despite their begging, I so far have declined to answer them. I told them that they had to wait until their early 20s before I shared those tales.

Unexpected deaths are a topic that physicians talk to one another about in private, soul-bearing sessions. Everyone dies, and all physicians are close to that fact. We learn it through years of training on the wards and in the early years of the deliberate practice of medicine.

Sometimes, it made me feel like a great novelist, an observer who had extraordinary insight into life, or a powerful public figure. Later it became more sobering and burdensome. These losses are less than beautiful, and they become more difficult to compartmentalize from ordinary life.

Let the healthcare system, fire department, police or coroner deal with it. That is society's necessary way of dealing with difficult and ugly situations.

In my specialty of EM, where the physician is not typically selected by their patient nor do they usually know very much about their patient, there is a continual hazard of the patient unexpectedly dying under your care or shortly after you have evaluated them.

I cared for an elderly man who presented with some vague abdominal pain that turned out to be a ruptured abdominal aortic aneurysm, a critical surgical emergency. I was able to diagnose, stabilize and then transfer the patient upstream to a surgeon. The patient then died in the OR.

This emergency was in marked distinction to his practitioner who had years – yes, years – to make a diagnosis on this easily screened-for disease. The time, scale and urgency make the ER a place of highs and lows, worry and threat, and not some place most patients choose to visit. These cases, as rarely as they occur, have a lasting impact and influence on the clinician. Simply said, they are just awful, gut-wrenching discoveries.

Becoming a physician is quite a process. We are exposed to things that are stunning, cannot really be understood, are too powerful to absorb, and too frightening to reach down and try to touch. When we first get started, we are still quite young ourselves, and we have little experience to provide context to cushion the fullness of a patient's life.

---

As an example, while working on the Saturday general surgery service at the county hospital during the early evening, I cared for a young man, then about my age in his mid-to-late 20s, who had suffered severe blunt trauma when struck by an automobile and was bleeding internally. He needed to be stabilized prior to going to the OR. One of the first steps was to start an IV.

Through this access, he could be given blood and other fluids that would keep him going until he could get to the OR. Back then, the technique was to cut down to the veins in the arm and then put the supply tube in under direct vision of the surgical site. There are slicker techniques now available.

While I was working on his elbow with great intensity to get this tube in place and save his life, he clawed his hand onto my arm, digging in with his nails and looked straight and deadly deep into my eyes.

"Am I going to die?"

There really was not much to say; his opportunities were dire, and I was highly focused on getting that IV started so there would be a chance to save his life. Don't look up, don't talk, just keep working.

He was going to die, and yet I replied, "No," while looking right into his eyes.

It did not make me feel good, but it was the right thing to do, and I would do it again. Shortly, despite the insertion of the IV and the fluids, he fell unconscious and died of blood loss right there, pale and gone.

---

In another case, an unmarried couple came to the ER and the woman's complaint was of a headache. I have seen many, many headaches and have become skilled in their evaluation. This headache was typical of a nonserious headache, and I knew right away she was seeking prescription pills.

The woman was correctly and diligently evaluated and given a small, appropriate amount of narcotic pain medicine. She was discharged from the ER with her significant other to care for her. All was well for a few hours. Then they returned, the headache was worse.

Again, I carefully evaluated her and did a neurological examination. The examination clearly indicated that she was under the influence of drugs, and I told the couple that she did not need any more pain medicine. They were told that she should not take any more drugs and should go home and rest.

Again, she was discharged with her significant other. I had a good feeling that I had not been manipulated twice that evening. The remainder of the long and tiring night shift was uneventful, and somewhere around 7:00 a.m. I crawled down to the dark, noisy, dirty call room to sleep until the cold and noise and my own circadian rhythm woke me up after about four hours of restless sleep. Even the heavy load of blankets, earplugs and a white-noise generator did not allow for much sleep down there.

As was my usual practice, I went back to the ER to see what problems remained, what errors had been made and to check in with the rest of the staff. Now, this morning was different. I was met with a swarm of people saying, "Do you remember that patient from last night? The one with the headache? She was brought to another hospital as a code blue and died in the ER!"

Dread and anxiety flowed over me like some awful thick immobilizing syrup. I felt a spike of acute depression.

I called the ER and talked with the treating physician who gave me a few more details, but he did not know too much.

The patient was pretty much dead on arrival and his evaluation and resuscitation did not add much as to the cause of death. Next, I called the boyfriend at home. There was extreme sorrow and consternation in his voice, but he was able to put the case together. There was no need to wait for the coroner.

After leaving the ER for the second time, they went home and she overdosed on her stash of available prescription drugs. He awoke in the early morning and found her unresponsive, not breathing and called the paramedics who delivered her to the ER, dead on arrival.

Weeks later, his story was confirmed by the result of the toxicology report from the coroner's office. That thick syrup of emotional heaviness went away. Would I have done anything differently? I don't know.

Perhaps I could have done an imaging study or an invasive test, like a lumbar puncture, to be especially certain that she did not have anything else going on. I believe she would have refused such studies, as was her right to do so.

In my judgment, she did not meet the requirement for nonvoluntary psychiatric detention, and she would have probably refused voluntary treatment. Not that we didn't know how dangerous drug misuse is, but this case again highlights how it can kill unexpectedly and in common ways.

———————

Another case from my trauma center days involved an elderly woman who had been knocked down in a crosswalk in the daytime and dragged by an automobile. She was brought to us with minimal signs of life and did not respond to any resuscitative measures.

After pronouncing her dead in the ER, I did my own mini postmortem exam. She died quickly and with too little response from our efforts. Something else was going on. Aside from multiple fractures, including the pelvis and long bones, the examination of her neck showed that she had suffered an atlanto-occipital (the top vertebrae connection to the head) dislocation.

Her head was dislocated or separated from her neck at the highest level and when I lifted her head, it came away in my hands, with no sense of being attached to the neck or the body. I was feeling the entire weight of her head in my palms, a very sad and disconcerting feeling. The lethality of the trauma was confirmed as well as the fruitlessness of our efforts. Our efforts in the ER were often impotent.

---

Another case involving an elderly woman illustrates the complications of being overweight and living with long-standing diabetes. She was inpatient because her blood sugar levels were too high, and she needed to have them more intensively managed.

She was very heavy, with slow and difficult movements. I had cared for her all night into the next day, and she was doing better. When I was at home that evening, I called in to see how she was doing. I had to wait on the phone while the staff attended to a patient in cardiac arrest.

Without being told who the patient was, I just instinctively knew that it was my patient. The staff was trying to resuscitate her, but she did not survive.

What happened? An autopsy determined that she had aspirated her stomach contents into her lungs and had basically drowned in her stomach juices.

I know now that her death might have been prevented if a tube had been placed in her stomach and the liquid contents sucked out. Had she been vigorous enough, and less heavy, she might have been able to lean forward and let the vomit go to the ground rather than back into her mouth. It is another case that I still feel sad about.

---

Sometimes it's one of our own. I knew two elegant, foreign-born brothers. They were physicians, about a year apart, one of whom I worked directly beside. The younger one was more friendly and ceaselessly joked with the other.

The older was previously married and now divorced with two young children. Well-groomed, stylish in a pressed white clinical jacket, he always had something going on and to look forward to. A full dance card. His younger brother, recently divorced without children, was a bit more casual. We enjoyed each other's banter and clinical insights. He was a colleague but was also a good friend and someone I looked forward to working with.

He would tease me, calling me his "second most favorite emergency medicine doctor," after his brother. He was a funny guy, and I loved it.

I worked Christmas that year. Returning in early January, I was stunned to learn that the older brother had died by suicide. With the care, thoroughness and determination that allowed him to become an excellent physician, he shot and hanged himself in the garage of the guest house where he lived on his parents' estate.

Mid-morning, on a busy day in the ER, I saw the younger brother enter the workstation area, and I hurried to his side. Wordlessly, I opened my arms and offered him a hug. He accepted. We hugged deeply for a long, very long period of time, so long that it attracted attention from coworkers. A remarkable *abrazo*, a man-to-man hug, we were on the verge of tears.

I invited him outside to the ambulance entrance for privacy. We talked and wondered and sighed. He shortly left the city for further education. I have known a lot of doctors and healthcare providers who have committed suicide.

———————

There was another doctor I got to know but not too well. He was about my age, maybe just a little younger, usually looking a little tired, probably from working all night. He was an OB-GYN. We didn't talk about cases too much or anything for that matter.

We started having breakfast together in the nearly empty cafeteria. I would just be starting my shift, sometime shortly after 7:00 a.m., and he usually would already be there, waiting for the next baby to be born.

He typically wore a simple plaid shirt and tie, and always had a book in his hand. Most of the time it was a paperback book, usually a mystery and frequently a murder mystery.

We made small talk about hospital politics and how they were messing up the place. Sometimes we talked about the problems of adequate nursing or the lack of nurses. We would also talk about collections and problems of collecting from the insurance companies or patients. This was just chit-chat to pass the time until the next time.

We did not talk about our families, our own business problems, or even our feelings. Maybe that was part of the problem.

The slow-moving rumor mill gave him lots of headaches. He had been divorced once and now was having problems with his second wife. He was an excellent physician and surgeon but had been involved in too many lawsuits, and now his partners were thinking of changing his status in the partnership because it would be too expensive to maintain his malpractice insurance relative to the revenues generated.

A reorganization it was called. He had been doing this sort of work for 25 years. It was his life; it had become him. That's all. These sorts of rumors persisted. I never asked nor discussed the things I heard about him at our irregular breakfasts, and they were never mentioned.

There were no signs of stress or discomfort. It was just like a typical man and even more like a physician to be so shut down and guarded. The last stories I heard about him were the worst, and they were not rumors.

Shortly after meeting with the partners, while his domestic unrest continued, the end came – suddenly and violently. He was at his own home in the privacy of his bedroom when he stabbed himself in his heart through his left ventricle, killing himself.

I can't really imagine what was going through his head at that time. He was a physician and surgeon with so many other options in life and knew many less painful ways to end his own life. It seems to me that it was a ritual death meant to communicate to all those still remaining that perhaps his work was his life and now that it was gone, he was gone, too.

It's difficult to know how someone feels with any degree of insight before having a conversation with them. Sometimes, the outside appearance does not reflect the inside. Just ask the poets and authors whose works detail those separations endlessly in literature.

Seeing someone who is highly respected with a seemingly enviable life take their own life, it's easy to wonder, "What went wrong?"

―――――――――

A slim, lean, pleasant, if not desperate woman around 40, with striking gray eyes, was brought in by the paramedics after neighbors heard gunshots. The courageous and tough woman had shot herself not once but twice! Both times in the left chest. She wanted to kill herself and was aiming for her heart. Both times she missed, giving herself a hemo-pneumothorax, a collapsed lung with bleeding into the collapsed lung space and a left breast, soft-tissue wound. She did not shoot a third time.

Upon arrival in the ER, she immediately looked deeply into my eyes and asked, "Doctor, where is my heart?"

The intensity, clarity and depth of that question took me by surprise. I looked deeply into those deadly gray eyes and chose not to answer. I didn't have the answer she was looking for.

―――――――――

A young man in the prime of life was brought in by the paramedics. Unfortunately, he did not have a painless death but ended up in a vegetative state instead. However, my job is not to philosophize about his fate but to treat and manage the patient.

He was posturing, which is a type of seizure where the brain is insulted by lack of oxygen. His dad's history told the story.

"I cut him down!" the father said through heaving tears. He had returned from an errand and found his son hanging by his neck from a rope the son had rigged in the garage. Not snapped, but strangulated, the tightness of the rope around the neck cut off blood and air to the head and the brain, and the results were now thrashing around on the gurney in front of me.

The fact that the patient was moving his extremities suggested that he did not have a serious injury to the bones and the tissues of the spinal cord. The bones in the neck needed to be checked out very carefully. With much effort from many nurses and X-ray technicians, he was moved to the radiology suite where the necessary X-ray films were taken, then reviewed and determined to be within normal limits and without injury.

Our goal now was to keep things from getting worse and to try and make them better. He was sedated, consulted and transferred to the ICU for further care and then psychiatric care if he did well enough.

Looking down at his puffy face, the red and blotchy whites of his eyes, the bruising of his neck where the rope had been and the highest functioning portion of his brain separated from the rest, 1 was filled with empty amazement and some despair at the behaviors and practices of our species.

The consultant in the hanging case was a neurosurgeon who was one of my favorite practitioners and was extremely personable. He was old school and had the ability to look around a room and make people comfortable under the most trying of circumstances. More often than not, they would become his friends. His bedside manner was friendly and easy-going, and the language he used put people at ease.

He was older and bigger than average size, with a distinctive abdomen. He did enjoy food and wine, and this was reflected in his face. With just a few words and non-verbal gestures from him, 1 felt better, and the family and patients felt better as well. This style spilled over into his personal life, and he was one of the most popular physicians on the medical staff. He was a wonderful person, physician and gentleman.

Insights can be powerful. Physicians sometimes know that the patient in front of them is about to die, and, even more rarely, the patients themselves know. Occasionally, both know. When I hear a patient say they are going to die, I take that premonition very seriously. Often, they are correct despite the advantage of the advanced warning and my best efforts to save them. The feeling some patients have of impending doom or death is pretty real.

A middle-aged man was brought to the ER by his wife for care one mid-morning. Heavyset and thick, his color was off, his skin was too dark. He had not been doing well all night and finally said it was time to be brought to the hospital. One seasoned look, and I knew there was no more that I could do for this patient.

As they say, he was a "wreck," and I was afraid that soon he would be "circling the drain." As I began this evaluation with the history, physical examination and obtaining the necessary laboratory and imaging studies, things got worse. His system started to unravel.

His blood pressure and heart rate started to go the wrong way, his oxygen levels dropped and he was getting loopy. He had difficulty following simple commands. He was having some multisystem malfunction and no clear diagnosis was in sight. This was not a problem – yet. I started correcting the things I knew I could work on. Fluids, drugs, more fluids and different drugs.

Now he developed a high fever, which was another very worrisome problem. We have antibiotics and plenty of them were pumped into the patient. Finally, things were doing a bit better after several hours of our work.

I would have loved to have transferred him to the ICU, but no one would have been able to see him promptly.

The patient was not stable, and I wanted him to remain under a physician's immediate care, so he remained in the ER.

I was one-on-one with him for hours, and he still maintained only the thinnest thread of stability, meaning he did not suffer a cardiac arrest. His wife explained he had a lot of medical problems, but she was not sure exactly what they were. If only I could talk to his always unavailable doctor.

This state of affairs continued for a while longer until it finally unraveled. The expected and unwanted cardiac arrest occurred, and there was nothing left to do except go through the effort of resuscitation. He was pronounced dead in the ER.

Awful. This was another one of those cases where the patient comes in talking and dies directly under my care. I went out to talk to the wife, and she was not surprised, only very sad. Then she told me that on the way to the hospital her husband told her that he was going to die.

Too many times I have had a patient say to me that they are going to die, and then, despite everything I do for them even in this modern setting, they do die, right in front of my eyes.

The expression of those feelings forebodes a very poor prognosis. I have heard it often enough to dread hearing those words myself. It is one of those things that contribute to the separation of EM physicians from the rest of medicine and from the great majority of nonmedical folk.

It is a contributor to the slow but corrosive posttraumatic stress disorder that develops in those who practice under these kinds of extreme conditions.

As an example, I have had more OB-related deaths than most OBs with a lifetime of practice, and the same would be said about the pediatric practice, neurology, etc. The ER is the place of the most sudden and disturbing deaths.

As might be said by United States Marine Corps combat soldiers, I have served my time in hell.

I have served my time in the ER, and it was time to get out and do something else.

## CHAPTER 16

# I LOVED
# BEING A HERO

One young adult patient's story contained all the elements of a real thriller: a beautiful young princess entering the bloom of her life, wonderful pink fuzzy slippers symbolic of her innocence and childhood, and a relentless ongoing electrical barrage within her young heart.

These factors were all perfectly arranged with the correct timing and intensity one special evening rather late in the ER. The stage was set. Instead of the usual busy ER with many patients competing for attention, it was very quiet.

Entering rapidly and very short of breath from a pathology in her heart conduction system, the dying heroine was pulled, dragged and carried along by two friends, then roughly put up on the gurney. The cardiac monitor showed a deadly fast heart rhythm. Her fine and beautiful heart was beating itself to death. Now, fortunately, this type of condition is easily treated by today's practice.

In a less-urgent situation, the condition is treated with medicines injected directly into the bloodstream for a rapid effect. In this case, since the situation was unstable and deadly, her heart needed a jolt of electricity. We gave it, and the results were textbook.

Her deadly heart rhythm was restored to the healthy normal one within seconds. Her heart rate slowed, her breathing normalized and her color returned. She was saved, plain and simple. We all heard imagined applause, long and loud.

In the commotion, one of the pink slippers had fallen off her foot. I felt like a prince when I bent down, picked it up and, with exaggerated care, placed it on her foot. A great case for its drama, finality, conclusion and poignancy. I loved being a hero.

Follow-up comes in many forms: directly from the patient or family, casual chats with the downstream physicians, review of the chart or, most commonly, nothing since most patients are lost to follow-up. The case and its identification are forgotten and lost to time.

The education and refining of a physician's judgment by reviewing past cases is a great way to continue to measure and remeasure our medical acumen. It illuminates the next patient's future by allowing us to do a better job in diagnosis and treatment. It is also a great feeling to see and know that we did the job right and saved someone's life.

The following demonstrates the necessity for prompt and correct action.

---

I could see the desperation in M.'s eyes. Wild, bulging and hungry for air. He was dying, and quickly. This scenario with M. had happened before and would happen again. He was always afraid. I had taken care of M. several times for his acute airway disease.

What would start as a mild asthma attack would very rapidly, within a minute or two, progress to completely difficult breathing. Imagine breathing normally and then suddenly trying to breathe through a cocktail-sized straw. M. was middle-aged, puffy, tall and softly overweight. When he had enough breath to talk, he was pleasant and knowledgeable enough to carry on an intelligent discussion about his disease. However, most of the time when we met, he was critically short of breath.

When I saw him come into the ER, I would grab the resuscitation equipment, run to him and start to rescue his airway. I had to work as hard and as fast as I could in order to save him. There was no room for error or misjudgment, and he would try to help by following my directions, breathing more slowly and opening his mouth as needed.

I would place a large-diameter tube into his main airway and then help him to breathe with a mechanical assist, all the while pumping his lungs and his body full of the strongest and most effective drugs I knew could help him to breathe again. It was a race against his mortal clock.

I was always able to stabilize him and get him safely to the ICU. This scenario was repeated multiple times, enough that I was able to get a sense of the man, his power and personality. I visited him in the ICU a few times and these follow-up visits were refreshing when I could see him as vigorous and in a normal state of mind.

I enjoyed seeing the results of my "save," and he enjoyed visiting with me. It was our tiny mutual admiration club. After some time when I had not seen him, I spoke to his attending pulmonary physician who told me that he had gone to another hospital and had not been successfully resuscitated. His death was not unexpected, he had many health issues; however, I was sad to learn of his passing.

Knowing how to manage a simple airway problem, stop bleeding and keep a heart going are all available techniques for every adult to learn. I heartily recommend learning them, and, with the same breath, I hope most people never have to use them.

Well-meaning bystanders who try to help an ill person represent a kinder and gentler aspect of the public than is usually displayed by citizens.

*He's having a heart attack!* These words of misdiagnosis, usually uttered in a restaurant by patrons as someone falls quite soundlessly into their soup or onto the floor, highlight the next case. This case was quite fantastic in that it demonstrated the three features of airway blockage and yet, still had a good outcome.

---

An older gentleman was enjoying a steak sandwich and a few whiskies in a local restaurant. It was in the late afternoon, and he was dining alone. He preferred his steak well-done. He had a history of dental neglect and now had upper dentures. He also had a history of cigarette smoking. He was hungry and eating quickly with large bites. The food smelled good, and he was feeling good, too. Suddenly that last big bite of steak did not go down. It got stuck. It got so stuck that he did not have time to dig it out with his hand or call for help. He just collapsed onto the floor.

Fortunately, a patron knew the Heimlich maneuver, and they used that skill multiple times until the paramedics arrived. They stabilized him and brought him to the ER. By then he was unconscious and blue. His once straight nose was totally smashed to the side. As the Heimlich was applied to this unconscious man, he flexed forward onto the counter with each compression, further displacing his nose. It was the most severe nasal fracture I had ever seen.

His airway needed immediate attention. Using the usual tools of the trade, including a specialized type of pliers,

I examined his throat, saw what the problem was and removed a piece of steak the size of my palm that was blocking his airway.

The Heimlich maneuver had opened the airway just enough that he did not die in transport to the hospital. As soon as the foreign body was removed, he began to pink up, and soon he was conscious and alert.

To deconstruct this case, his long history of cigarette smoking gave him less breath-holding time in which to try to save himself. His drinking caused impaired judgment and coordination, which made him less competent to save himself. The dentures did not allow him the proper feel of food in his mouth and the size of the uncut piece of meat put his case over the edge. He was admitted for observation, did well and had an ear, nose and throat (ENT) specialist fix his nose.

There are wonderfully dramatic cases from a medical standpoint that are easy – basically a chance for the physician to be a hero.

---

Imagine the excitement and exhilaration of running through a construction site in the dark, leaping and jumping around. Like dancing in the dark, exciting and a bit forbidden.

Then imagine the sickening feeling of falling and having something large pierce the back of your head, that area just below the skull where the neck joins the scalp.

You struggle to get up, find you are unable and start to scream for help. You feel fear and then sheer terror. The paramedics are somehow called and find you with the point of a pitchfork through the back of your neck. From a medical point of view, all of this is of slight importance. No major organs, important cosmetic or functional areas are injured or destroyed.

Carefully and painfully you are loaded into an ambulance, transported to the ER and soon greeted by the trauma team. A fantastic presentation of bodily injury. It is the kind of case ER doctors love.

A physician promptly recognizes that your injury will have a good outcome and sees in their mind's eye to the end of the healing process. Thus, a chance to be a hero and for a moment feel the power of knowledge and experience.

The doctors huddle, get another consultation and proceed to act. Suddenly, and rather abruptly, they inject the medicine directly into the muscle, and then they reach down and pull this pitchfork spike out of the back of your neck.

You are then taken to the OR for a more formal exploration and repair. After a few days, you are well enough to go home. From a medical standpoint, this was an easy case without a large amount of tissue damage, as no important structures were injured. There is a good outcome, everyone is happy and sometimes one of our "saves" becomes the stuff of legends.

---

In another case, the patient suffered a rapidly collapsing airway management problem. The original attending physician was only too happy to let me take over.

We don't use nasotracheal intubation often (this was before the now common action of sedation and paralysis prior to intubation in the ER setting), so when one of the younger members of our group struggled with a patient suffering from severe shortness of breath, I was glad to show my younger colleagues one more trick to save a life.

The patient was huge – read 375-plus pounds – and he was struggling to breathe. The stress on the MD's face was as severe as the patient's, and I noticed the worrisome calm of the situation in that treatment room.

With the confidence based on years of practice, and a practical depth of knowledge from many similar desperate encounters, I easily intubated the patient by the nasotracheal route.

Once that critical intervention was completed, the patient was sedated and paralyzed, and the tube secured, everyone relaxed. The crisis was over. This was a lesson well-taught and well-received.

When my younger colleague told me that he had mentioned the story to another younger physician to show that the older guys "knew something," a tiny bit of legend had been created, and I liked the feeling. But not every "save" is seen as heroic.

———————

I have a strong recollection of the next case and its outcome; the results of my efforts were apparent in the eyes and behavior of the patient's mother. I now know the gist of what happened based on the history obtained.

It was summertime in SoCal, and a toddler was brought in by the paramedics as a near-drowning case. No one knew how long the baby had been in the water. The baby was now limp and blue but still had a heartbeat. We began a resuscitation that was successful.

The child improved enough to make it to the pediatric ICU and was finally discharged. The child, now home, was not the same child who fell into the water.

Six years later I saw the child again. He was now about eight years old. The mom brought him to the ER in the early evening with a fever that needed diagnosing and treating, which was a routine, no big deal kind of case.

The mother then looked meaningfully at me and said, "You're the doctor who saved my baby."

I nodded and said, "Yes."

The child was not normal and never would be. He was cognitively disabled and spastic, stiff, with roaming eyes that could not process what was going on around him. We talked for a while about generalities, the current diagnosis, its treatment and how long I had been working in the ER. The way she looked seldomly at her child, did not comfort him affectionately and some of the words she used let me know her feelings about her relationship with the boy. He had become a loved object rather than a growing and curious child.

Though medically I had done the right and correct thing, perhaps it was not right for her.

The sadness in her eyes showed that the outcome was an awful burden for her and her family. All of that modern, fancy knowledge and equipment did not make anyone better or happier, and her pain would last forever.

The ambiguity of a situation like this left me feeling disquiet, like somehow I had not done the best thing for that family. I yearned for medically simpler times with more of an all-or-none outcome.

––––––––––––

It has been said that "self-praise stinks" and that certainly applies to ER physicians. Doing our most earnest and sometimes best efforts on the unconscious and seeing them survive and start to recover in the ICU is the stuff of legends, TV shows and hero-making. It does make one feel good but missing from the "atta boys" is any thank you from the unconscious patient.

A patient may awaken in the ICU with a tube down their throat, a couple of serious IV lines in their body and tubes in their chest. It's common not to have any memory of these events and therefore have no recognition of the lifesaving events in the ER.

Weeks later a bill may arrive from some insurer or medical group for far too much money. The patient may think, *Hey, what is this bill for? I don't remember needing any of this!* In any case, an ER physician is accustomed to little thanks from patients.

Of course, it is ironic we do our best work on unconscious patients, those folks who have entered a space between here and there and need a hand. I am glad to say that, more often than not, we are able to push them into consciousness. They often wake up and regain consciousness in another part of the hospital and have little to no recollection of how they got there.

It is as though an invisible but powerful force pushes the severely ill patient into a safer harbor. The ER as a team is that force: powerful, ready and present at all times.

ER folk have been called miracle workers.

Do we mind? Well, of course, we mind, but that is just the way it is, and it will not change. It is a real pleasure to get a compliment. Even a simple compliment from one patient can make us smile and feel good inside.

———

A patient offered a real sense of appreciation for the work we do while I was off duty and not involved in the care. It was generic, for all the frontline emergency caregivers.

It happened outside of the hospital while I was on vacation with my family in Yellowstone National Park in the state of Wyoming. Lounging in a log cabin interpretive center near a pool of geysers, we struck up a conversation with a man about my age, in his late 50s, who told of his experiences in the park. He'd been attacked by a grizzly bear, and he had the scars to prove it, which he showed me.

Some years ago, with friends, he was dropped off in a remote area of the park. He was very well-equipped with food and supplies, including an excellent medical aid kit, and he was a knowledgeable, small-animal veterinarian from Massachusetts. Early on in the trip, he was savagely attacked so quickly he did not have time to spray the bear with the repellent he always carried.

Curled up in a ball, he was bitten, clawed and then thankfully left alone. It took 22 hours to get him out of there. During this time, he self-managed, self-medicated and did a good job of it until he was brought to a full-on care facility and seen by a good ER physician.

There must have been a real sense of relief and protection upon arrival to that ER department. He still had kind and excellent feelings for the attending physician who cared for him. From a strictly medical standpoint, there were not so many medical or surgical needs going on at that point that needed emergency care.

However, when I told him that I did that kind of work, too, he was delighted. He wanted to thank me and to be able to thank all those who work in the ER. He was quite effusive. The company that manufactures bear repellent spray legitimized his story by using him in their advertisements. He inscribed a copy of the company's brochure with these words of praise and handed it to me: *Paul, ER docs made me well. Thanks for what you do. T.*

More stuff of legends.

Hearing his story, touching his wounds and feeling his deep gratitude reminded me that being an ER doctor was a rewarding path. Sometimes, patients who have experienced heightened helplessness and encountered their darkest fears are especially thankful, and it is satisfying to receive those thanks.

---

It is one thing to get praise from the public or the nonmedical staff, but it always feels particularly good to receive thanks from the pros.

In one situation, I was called to the OR, which is never a good sign because the ER is the place where I belong. Having to be moved off base suggested to me that things were not going well.

I had been called into one of the ORs to help a general surgeon with whom I had a common working relationship. We would exchange a "hi" and "how's it going" in passing but nothing more. This time, there was stress in his voice and eyes as he asked me to give him a hand in obtaining IV access for the patient he had recently operated upon and who was now going into severe shock. I figured this was due to blood loss of some kind.

In any case, I immediately went into the OR. It was time for action, not words, so I kept working and did not look up as I finally started a very large IV portal in the patient's groin. Now the surgeon had a chance of keeping up with the blood loss. I could see the surgeon calm down now that we had a "line."

The surgeon thanked me, and I left the OR. After the case was finished, he made it his business to visit the ER to thank me again. It was my move that saved the day. It felt good that he appreciated my skill and effort.

A year or so later, that surgeon, who was a cigarette smoker, did not show up at work one morning and was discovered dead in his bed at home, where he lived alone. He probably died of a cardiac event.

Another physician I worked with had the look of a gladiator. His body was square and very muscular with a thick neck, arms and legs, and a bear-like chest, but the tip-off was two cauliflower ears, the kind people only get from hard fighting in hand-to-hand combat. Looking more closely, he had dense scar tissue above each eyebrow, which was also from trauma. His manner, however, was very different from his appearance.

He was deeply humble. He did not want to bother me about the long and deep wound above his lateral right eyebrow. He had gotten the wound a few hours earlier while training for a mixed martial arts "cage fight." The wound was still giving him problems and had continued to bleed.

The surgical management of this wound was relatively simple: anesthetize, clean and repair. It was a no big deal, run-of-the-mill case.

However, this physician was on our medical staff and well respected. He did not want to trouble me while I was working the ER where more important and serious cases needed to be taken care of. Again and again, he absolutely refused my suggestions, offerings and advice to have this wound correctly managed with sutures. He would only allow me to tape it closed.

I did this following a period of chatting and some joking around. The wound closed up quite well with the careful tape job, and it healed just fine. The cosmetic effect was very satisfactory.

He was disproportionately thankful for my effort and was always saying how much he liked the result. In some way, he represented one end of the spectrum of vanity. The other end might be represented by a family that requested a plastic surgeon.

In another situation, a mother cried, "I don't care what it costs!" regarding her beautiful infant daughter who suffered a quarter-inch wound beneath the chin, a wound that would never have any social consequences. There was a great contrast between that physician's humble manner and that of the infant's mother.

Appreciation is not always needed, though. A younger Hispanic male, pale with pain and fright, was brought into the ER by the paramedics and was surrounded by a group larger than necessary. I knew by the size of the onlookers that it would be a horrific type of case.

On the gurney, the patient's right hand and forearm were not visible but encased inside a gray aluminum meat grinder.

Sadly, while working, his hand had gotten caught into the pulverizing screw mechanism of the grinder. The extremity was caught and ground up to the extent that it could not be pulled out. It was firmly stuck.

The first order of business was to free the extremity from the machine's grip. Simultaneously, while we called the maintenance department, the patient received a powerful intravenously administered drug to numb him and take the pain away. The call to maintenance was for a tool to turn and back out the screw mechanism to free his arm; it was too wedged in to just pull it out. When the patient was relaxed and feeling no pain, the screw direction was reversed, and the forearm and hand were freed.

The machine had done what it was supposed to do. The extremity was now ground meat. In medical terms, there were multiple fractures, shattered bones, lacerations, and a partial amputation with torn and hanging skin muscle, blood vessels and nerves. It was obvious that amputation was needed and later that evening it was done by the orthopedics in the OR. Recovery from the amputation was uneventful, and the patient was discharged.

Later, perhaps years later, while I was going through the cafeteria line of a high-end health club, I saw the same man behind the counter making one-armed smoothies – quite a neat trick – for the patrons who belonged to the club.

I did not talk to him because I did not need recognition, praise, thanks or want any resentment, and he gave no recognition of me. Due to the medications and the excitement of the night, it was unlikely he would recognize me anyway. Such is life.

# CHAPTER 17

# BLOODY
# LAUNDRY

At the end of the shift, there is the dirty laundry to deal with, and I don't mean the social kind, I mean the stuff that comes from the upfront and personal exercise of delivering healthcare to patients.

Imagine, if you dare, the feeling at the end of a day as you change out of your clothes soiled with the blood from the patients you were working on.

Too often, after being pressed up against trauma patients, working with them and dealing closely with their wounds, volumes of their blood are spilled upon you. Despite protective gear, it can filter its way through.

This always makes me want to take a long, hot shower right then and there. I can't feel clean enough too soon, and I have always just thrown stained clothing away. There is too much closeness and grossness.

Remembering that medicine is an ancient profession with its origins based in the primitive darkness of early humans' grief and pain, and its ability to ease these discomforts, it makes sense for us to deliver comfort at life and death moments.

Patients want to hear it from the "man," the boss, the doctor, the physician, and no one else will do. The tone, body posture, choice of words, language and every facet of verbal and nonverbal communication are carefully noted and remembered by the anxious and stressed patient or their families. They may not remember the complete details of the message, but they will understand its direction and content.

The responsibility of the delivery of bad news often falls upon the EM physician as team leader – and no one else wants to do it. After a while, each physician develops their own style.

During my training, there was no education in this matter, just the observation of seniors doing it, and, at some point, we each had our own chance to deliver the news.

Later on, in the evolution of EM, a more formal process to deliver bad news in the best and kindest way was developed. The content was of less importance than the body language, tone of speech, manner and timing.

During a fruitless resuscitation, I would often quickly go out and tell the waiting family what the situation was and let them know that things were not going well. Then finally, when it was over, the news was not shocking but confirming.

This lessened the blow and allowed the raw process of grieving to begin. Other times, the information was a confirmation, and the family knew that the person was dead already. They just needed to hear it from the physician.

In these cases – as in the elderly, cancer patients, suffering people, the worn-out and emotionally exhausted – families tended to receive this news with acceptance and thanks.

At other times, people have literally torn their hair out from their scalps on hearing the bad news. They have thrown themselves prostrate upon the floor and writhed about in their grief, grief that was so palpable it made me want to flee. I did not want to see, hear or be around those kinds of powerful emotions. It was haunting.

Haunting in that I still remember the disintegration of a family right before my eyes after I attended to a child who died when their head was run over by a parent.

Who can imagine the reverberations of that kind of family event or would want to think about it much? Occasionally, the deaths we witness or confirm are calming and peaceful, but once I had a family and children of my own, these cases tore me up inside and continued to roll around in my head, disturbing a nice thought I was having.

An unexpected, out of the blue, uncommon, worrisome or even deadly diagnosis can present at any time in someone who arrives at the ER expecting a simple diagnosis.

Though rare, uncommon occurrences do make their way onto the diagnostic scorecard for the unfortunate few. In most communities, a cancer diagnosis is made by office-based providers: family medicine, internal medicine and the internal medicine subspecialties. Broadly speaking, the more prosperous the community, the less cancer is diagnosed in the ER, and the reverse is true. When I was working in a very poor and underserved area, I would make a diagnosis of cancer all too often.

---

I recall such a case one Saturday morning in the busy time of day in the beautiful spring of Southern California. A father brought his teenage son to the ER who had been seen at the university hospital a week or so earlier for a shoulder pain believed to be related to a sports injury but was not getting any better. The father was requesting a second opinion. He also noted that his son was looking a bit "peaked." It was really a pretty simple case.

I asked the patient if moving his shoulder made the pain worse, and he said no. This strongly suggested that the pain was not in the shoulder and was coming from a less apparent location, which is known as referred pain. In this case, it was coming from the diaphragm, and most likely from an enlarged spleen.

The history and the dad's comments were enough to strongly suggest leukemia, and this was confirmed by ordering a simple blood test, which showed an abnormally high number of white blood cells and a low number of red blood cells resulting in the pale, "peaked" appearance noted by the father. What a case.

I was so sorry to be the bearer of this news, such savagery of biology and life. News like this would take anyone by surprise and can be startling. It's difficult to know what will come along or what is next. The endlessly flowing river of life through the ER is able to sweep all those in its path into the sea of despair or death.

As a physician, we must remember that we did not cause the disease; we are merely the service provider, the healer, the bearer of the news and the provider of hope. The river continues, and it will either wash those in its path clean or wash them away.

A quiet ER is usually an efficiently run shop. The disruption of a screaming, or a screaming and combative patient, is unsettling to the other patients and staff. Care is fragmented, and delays and errors can always creep into the system. It is hard to have a happy ER, but quiet and ordered are doable, and the results are worth the extra efforts by the staff.

---

Imagine a violently struggling, robust man in the prime of his life blessed with great strength trying to rid himself of three burly police officers who want him to have a medical examination.

This occurred at an inconvenient hour in the ER when we were busy with many patients. The man was brought in screaming profanities and doing everything he could to get away to destroy the place and all its people. He needed to be restrained but without hurting him or preventing him from breathing, which would only create more problems.

While this wild man was trying to get away, the nursing staff attempted to dart him with a powerful tranquilizer while avoiding accidentally injecting someone else.

Finally, a bare arm was available for injection. There, it was swiftly pushed in.

I noticed that he had a tattoo of a serpent on the same arm, so I leaned in close and whispered in his ear, "The stuff we just gave you is just like venom, and the more you struggle, the quicker it will get to you."

Instantly, and I mean instantly, he stopped fighting and moving, relaxed and was then firmly placed into handcuff restraints. The dose of medicine and its pharmacologic trajectory would not have had an immediate effect as I had observed. This was 100% mental power, an extraordinary example of the placebo effect.

Cases received at the trauma center, in the 4:00 to 5:00 a.m. time of day, are when the sun is just coming up and the desperate and deeply drunk return, creature-like, to the places they inhabit during the day.

---

A patient, who was a little older than middle-aged, was brought in after being the at-fault driver in a serious motor vehicle accident.

She had caused the accident that had killed three people at the scene, dead on arrival, so they were not even brought to the hospital. Her injuries were not serious – minor wounds to the face and hands, that was all. Her concern was for her pet. She kept exclaiming, "Who will take care of my dog?" That was her reality.

My feelings toward this lady took me to some very dark places of my mind. It was very hard not to be judgmental toward her. I felt that had she been seriously injured, I could have watched her bleed to death with no concern or remorse.

This struck me as similar to the feelings I imagine soldiers in battle would feel toward their enemies. I didn't even know I had such strong feelings inside of me.

Where did they come from? I might as well have asked where it all got started. The feelings were real and so was the situation. I always hope that the next time, it is easier to feel neutral toward these types of patients and have fewer of those dark feelings. The late 19th-century physician, Sir William Osler, put a premium on equanimity, "A state of calmness and observation that allowed one to act correctly in situations of stress and urgency."

This is a good mantra to remember in the ER, but sometimes it can be difficult. There was no calmness and coolness within me at that time. It would not be the last time I met such intense feelings and thoughts in my ER practice.

Those dark feelings do not help in doing the work. They get in the way of the job, distracting from the task. On the other hand, they are reminders of the humanity within all of us. Being able to feel emotions is quite precious and should not be extinguished even within the darkest moments of ER practice.

That tension is demonstrated by the ceaseless comments about patients, their conditions and their lifestyles by the staff and physicians. In fact, all who care for patients on a daily basis, from radiology techs to phlebotomists, are full of comments about the folks who are under their care. It is a coping mechanism.

Gossip is the currency of hospital life. Privacy is replaced by gossip, and it is not really about who our patients are as humans but simply comments on the condition of the flow of life and passage through the system.

From the practitioner's point of view, the patient becomes the diagnosis. A single diagnosis, or one of many, determines a patient's care and probably their outcome. It is convenient and a shortcut, which avoids the need to personalize.

Once a diagnosis has been designated, the treatment follows according to the treatment paradigm of the caregivers, and the treatment plan of the day, week, year or decade, changing based on so many things, from basic research to the political economics of the institution.

That last lecture or paper read by one of your caregivers will be burning a hole in their head trying to get out and into a patient's care portfolio.

There is medical progress, but it is not smooth and proceeds by many small steps and fallbacks. However, there is progress, and it can be measured. The statistics measure the advances. Everyone loves anecdotal evidence and stories. It is easy to relate to an anecdote and that usually makes us feel at ease. There is just so much more to have a good personal feeling about, rather than a review of the data.

Occasionally the role of the ER physician extends to that of a grief counselor. When a patient dies in the ER, the family is told of the death, nursing and administration offer support and logistic plans, and the flow of patients through the ER continues. The work must go on. Rarely do we make any contact with the family after the death of the patient.

I was working at the trauma center when in the midafternoon a young man, in his early 20s, was brought in with a self-inflicted single gunshot wound to his head. Medically speaking, it was an easy case, low stress. This patient would die no matter what.

We performed the basics of resuscitation and kept the patient comfortable, but soon he died. The bullet had done too much damage to his brain. He had been at a local indoor handgun firing range when he suddenly, and impulsively, put the gun to his head and fired, killing himself.

I had been to that same range and knew exactly where the episode had happened. Other than being so close to such ugliness, the case was not really eventful for me. However, about one year later, after eating lunch in the doctors' dining room and just leaving to go back to work, I was approached by a quite ordinary appearing, pleasant middle-aged woman dressed normally, carrying a handbag. I did not sense any threat.

"Are you the doctor who cared for my son? He shot himself at the gun range."

"Yes," I replied. Now I was worried that not only had this lady tracked me down to a relatively private area of the hospital but had also correctly identified me without any introduction and had some questions about her son's death. The questions were not about medical management or quality of care but about her son and the quality of life in his last minutes and moments.

"Was he all right? Was he suffering? Did he say anything?"

I relaxed but still could not stop looking at her hands. I was concerned for my personal safety, and I searched for weapons. This mom had only one thing on her mind, however, and that was closure. The one-year anniversary of his death was close at hand, and she needed to get these deeply personal questions answered, and they needed to be answered from a primary source – me.

Fortunately, and gladly, I was able to answer her questions, reassure her and put her mind to rest. I could see that worry and tension left her as I told her that her son did not suffer, did not feel anything and had an easy death. Her worry and torment were over. It was odd to have that type of deep intimacy with someone suddenly and abruptly, completely and finally.

Such is the practice of EM.

---

Touch as a diagnostic modality is many centuries old. It makes up for its lack of modernity with safety, rapidity, simplicity, reliability, convenience and cost.

I continue to use it on all sorts of cases with excellent reliability and results. Consider the following: the ease of diagnosis of a hot boil, the abnormal movement of bone ends grinding across each other diagnosing a fracture, lightly feeling air beneath skin suggesting all sorts of concerning problematic diagnoses, the expected abnormality of a dislocated joint and the many qualities of a pulse.

So much information is available to the fingertips that even feeling different vibrations through the chest wall suggests different problems. Old school by two centuries or more, touch is quick, informative and safe.

Touching is different now than at the beginning of medicine. Then there was a sacred and privileged meaning to the movement of the hands on the patient. New, and a little bit frightening and forbidden, touching was allowed and encouraged.

People had special areas to be examined, touched and shared only with their physicians. I don't mean the genitals.

———————

As an example, I had the privilege as a physician of being allowed and, more than that, encouraged to examine the inside of a woman's face that had been eaten away by an ENT cancer. I could look from her eyeball socket straight into her mouth.

The prosthesis kept the world away from that view and gave her a sense of fullness and completeness that was taken away from her by a cure. She seemed pleased and comforted when I asked her to remove her prosthesis, then I stuck my finger into that cavity and explored the void clean and free of disease.

This was a comfort for her and a new sense of touch for me. As a younger physician, touching initially was easy and frequent and then later in my practice, I felt that the patients were more like contagions, and I touched them less. I never felt that they were too infectious, but the use of gloves as a common article of practice did put a barrier between the easy earlier days of touching.

Also, the need for speed and the knowledge base of practice did away with the need to touch. That is, I could faster and more easily get the same diagnosis without the blurring of the intimacy and need of touch. It is unfortunate for the patient that touch, perhaps the most basic healing process that the physician has to offer, now is one of the least useful in the diagnostic process.

The therapeutic side of things is another matter. Of course, almost everyone likes to be touched, particularly by a healing arts practitioner; it just makes us feel good. The EM practice with its need for diagnosis, and I mean diagnosis with a capital D, does not allow for the healing time and disrespects the healing value of touch, unfortunately.

All ER time is spent in extracting a diagnosis from the patient by using the system tools to the maximum and costliest degree. Healing is not part of the equation of healthcare. Too many patients present without a clear diagnosis and will never receive the needed touch.

I also feel that in my case there was a lessening of my ability to give and heal over the years of my practice. I felt at some level I was sharing too much of myself when I touched patients. I did not have enough emotional and therapeutic reserve to share. I had become an obligated volume operator in the healthcare system. My position in the stream of caregiving was well on the way to becoming one of the human machines that did the work of collecting data for a diagnosis. I did not want to touch patients anymore.

Hand washing eventually became a welcome ritual, a 26-second time-out from work to enjoy the pleasant feel of soap and water, and a sense of relief that I was not a transmitter of disease to the next patient.

The infectious disease physicians were so careful about regularly washing that in one case, one of them washed his hands carefully before and after consultation when he did not even touch the patient at all.

Now, I like to touch my pets and farm animals, and hug my family. The fur and flesh are nice to feel, and I do not worry about medical or biological concerns. Though it still is kind of fun to thump out the boundaries of an enlarged organ. Very old school.

––––––––––––

The zit on my back was not getting any better. Now after a few days, it was as "sore as a boil" and twice as big, about the size at its base of a quarter, burrowing its way into my shoulder blade area. This painful sore was not going away without medical intervention. And that intervention was surgery.

The boil, abscess or carbuncle needed lancing, incision, drainage, release and extraction of all that pus. I saw it as an opportunity to be on the other side of the table. I would go to the ER, act like a patient and get it taken care of on my next shift. Fortunately, my next shift was a daytime one so when I showed up at 7:00 a.m., the ER probably would not be crowded, and I could get it taken care of without delay or staff inconvenience.

Inconvenience? No way. The nursing staff was delighted to have a chance to operate on this ole doc. I bet I could have auctioned off the chance to do the job.

Playing the role of a loudly complaining patient complete with wild gestures and the, "I can't take it anymore!" screams, we all went into a treatment room. I whipped off my top and dramatically threw it on the floor saying, "You have got to give me relief!"

I pretended to struggle while four nurses held me down and tried to calm and comfort me.

"It won't hurt!"

"It's for your own good!"

"Everyone is like this!"

"We've seen it before!"

"Don't be afraid!"

"Be a big boy!"

I stopped struggling long enough for them to spray some really cold analgesic called Vapocoolant on my back and when it was "numb," they stabbed it with a needle or a scalpel. I then heard them scream as a stream of putrid, foul-smelling pus blew out of the wound. They all jumped back fast except the last one, who got some of that awful stuff on her hand. It was over, and I no longer struggled.

I had learned to love the healthcare delivery system. Soon they had applied a dry, sterile dressing to the wound, and I was released out of the ER and back into society. I really did not understand or even remember the aftercare instruction they had given me. I was so relieved it was over.

The boil or abscess soon healed, and it was merely a story to be told. However, I recalled the fun and adventure of that incident for many years, told and retold it to the new staff members until it became something of a dull but humorous ER urban legend.

"Remember when we operated on Doctor Weinberg? What a ..."

This would not be the only time I would also play the patient.

One evening, early on in the practice of EM, when I was moonlighting at different ERs around Los Angeles, I had been having run-of-the-mill back pain, but it had been going on for long enough that I thought I should seek out medical treatment.

Instead of going to a physician, I decided that I could take care of it myself.

Wrong.

I started with a lumbosacral X-ray, an important tool for seeing what was wrong with the bones but not the right thing to do for back pain in a patient of my age and circumstances.

From a position of privilege, during a quiet time, I asked the X-ray tech to do the films. He gave me the films, and I put them up on the view box to review them. They were well done and of good quality, the angles were all correct, but there were one or two spots in the low back that did not look right to me.

In fact, they looked bad, so bad that I knew that I had diagnosed a usually fatal blood condition in myself. I was suddenly weak and nauseous, exhausted and depressed, wrung out and used up. To say the least, it was awful to see those lesions. I wanted to curl up into the fetal position and go away.

I continued working that night, but it was so hard to do my duty when I had this diagnosis on my own mind. It was hard to concentrate and to even talk because I was having an acute grief reaction. I was single and free of any significant relationships at the time, not even a cat. I knew my family would be devastated but supportive.

Finally, the shift was over. The radiologists would be coming into the hospital for the start of their day in a little while, and I could get a second opinion on the films. I was too messed up to even eat breakfast, so I just laid down in the call room until they arrived.

At the end of my shift, I made my way into the radiology suite with the films in my hand. As casually as possible, I snapped the films into the view box.

"What do you think of these?" I said quickly and then waited. The experienced radiologist took just an instant to look at the films and pronounced them normal.

"What's the problem?" he asked.

Boldly, I pointed to those troublesome lesions that I had seen the previous night.

"They're nothing," he said, looking at me quizzically.

He then gave them some long medical name that I could not remember, and I was dismissed. I thanked him. I never told him that he was reading my films.

Of course, I felt great relief. However, the deeper feelings of impending death took some time to go away. I believe it was some months until the feeling was completely gone.

The personal nature of the situation had burned itself into my brain and it took time to make it go away.

I shared the story with several medical friends who listened and gave no special comments. It was a small case filled with errors. I had been spared, but then again, I was one of the lucky ones.

It is always a bit special for me to care for other medical doctors. We know each other too well. The commonality of medical school and early training years create a base of irreversible transformation into caregivers. There was a special sort of troubled privilege for the one in the healing role.

―――――――――

S. was grumpy, eccentric, a bit aloof, knowledgeable and compassionate. He would walk next to the wall along the corridors of the hospital in the usual lanes and would not always acknowledge others when they said, "Hello." He had patients with difficult problems, wounds that would not heal, all potentially reversible but in practice the most difficult to manage and treat. This was a tough practice for a somewhat troubled physician.

Still, I liked him and felt saddened when he was diagnosed with a very serious cancer and its treatment started to wear him down. It was then that he came to the ER for treatment. At once I knew things were not good.

Pale and sweating with intense pain, he needed a bed and right away. He gave me the diagnosis: a strangulating hernia. There on his right side was the lump and it was giving him so much pain. Treatment for that kind of condition is usually to push the lump back in and the strangulating pain is quickly relieved. If the hernia has been out too long, then the patient needs surgery.

Surgery may also become necessary if we cannot get the lump back in. He had much experience in reducing the hernias of his patients. The ER was extremely busy that day with all kinds of unstable patients and patients with life-threatening problems.

S. was cool and collected, and after I started an IV and gave him the full and potent dose of IV narcotic, he started relaxing.

"S., why don't you do it? I'll be right back," I said. I had other more worrisome patients to see.

Well, he easily reduced his own hernia. He had put his knowledge and his own skilled hands to good use.

He was relieved, and so was I. He was discharged from the ER and was on his way again. Sadly, and not unexpectedly, the cancer progressed. S. heroically continued to work and help his patients despite his weight loss and hair loss. He kept at it until he was too ill to serve his patients effectively.

That type of courage and toughness is all too rare and will be missed.

# CHAPTER 18

# LEAVING

The last case I had before retirement was a newborn, three weeks old, with a fever and no other symptoms. He had a history of viral exposure to chickenpox from family members, and his dad had a common cold. The workup did not reveal anything, and, after consultation with neonatology, the agreed plan was to send him home.

When I called to check on him in the morning, I found that he had been admitted. Something had changed or someone was more worried.

Saved? I don't know and didn't want to find out. This was just another one of those difficult cases that kept me humble and on my toes.

One of our excellent younger emergency physicians gave me a big hug at the end of the shift as I picked up my kit and prepared to walk out. He asked when he would see me again.

"Come to Paso Robles," I said.

There wasn't much emotion after all. It was past 2:00 a.m. and I was tired and ready to get out of there. I knew

I would be back in a few hours to clean up the paperwork, eat lunch and get ready to go home. What could I really say that hadn't been said before, particularly after close to a full and complete 30 years?

Tired, but not wasted, trashed or otherwise totally used up, the last shift ended with a whimper and not a bang.

I washed my hands and walked away.

THE END

# ABOUT
# THE AUTHOR

As a Woodstock-rocking baby boomer, Paul Weinberg's adventurous practice in medicine was an easy career choice to make. Learning the intricacies of medicine and surgery opened up many opportunities for him to interact with the lives of a broad range of people.

After graduating from the Keck School of Medicine of the University of Southern California and training at one of the largest teaching hospitals, Los Angeles County-USC Medical Center, his life path unfolded.

He was fortunate to have the opportunity to practice medicine in many parts of the world. He practiced from the mountains of New Guinea and Indian health service sites to remote parts of the Western states to Arctic villages. He also practiced in the American Samoa in Polynesia and the Virgin Islands. He has practiced in underfunded inner-city neighborhoods, and rural sites to urban and suburban medical centers and trauma centers. He has also practiced as a ship's physician and cared for those in the broken, narcotics-ravaged towns in the eastern US.

The diseases were mostly similar and sometimes rare. Dr. Weinberg tailored the delivery of care to the population based on each region's culture, paying close attention to local rules of practice, with their particular knowledge, tradition and experience. His method of delivery was often a long way from the style of the academic centers.

Dr. Weinberg learned a great deal from his patients and the local practitioners, and, delightfully, the path continued to unfold.

He currently resides on a ranch in California wine country with his wife, a small pack of dogs, horses and Longhorn cattle. He has two grown daughters and enjoys horse riding in his free time.

*(Left)* From ER doctor to cowboy. "Living the dream."

*(Bottom)* The doctor-turned-cowboy at home on his ranch with his wife Stacie and Bear, a rescued Great Pyrenees.

(*Top*) Dave Stein and Bob Cockrell (L to R). Just an outing with the guys. What could possibly happen here? (Cue the foreboding suspense music.) Hopefully all the protective gear will keep us from becoming yet another story in any future book.

(*Bottom*) Taking a break from bicycle riding. Note the obligatory helmet (Dave). Those lessons from 30 years in the ER follow me everywhere.